MEDIEVAL CHURCH AND CHURCHYARD MONUMENTS

Sally Badham

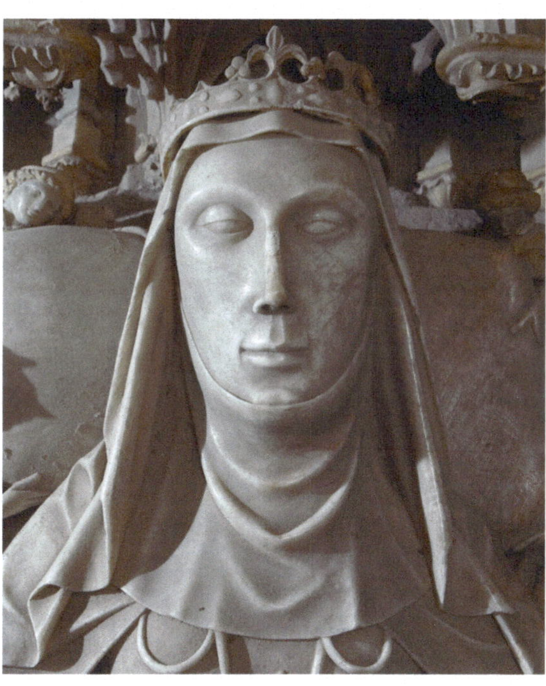

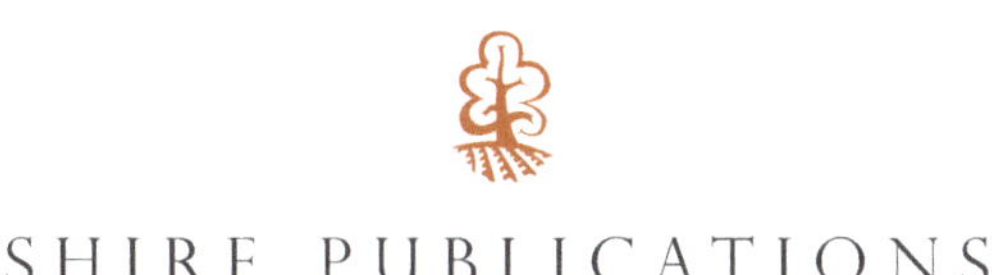

SHIRE PUBLICATIONS

Published by Shire Publications Ltd,
PO Box 883, Oxford OX1 9PL, United Kingdom.
PO Box 3985, New York, NY 10185-3983, USA.
E-mail: shire@shirebooks.co.uk   www.shirebooks.co.uk

© 2011 Sally Badham.
First published 2011.

Transferred to digital print on demand 2015.

All rights reserved. Apart from any fair dealing for the purpose of private study, research, criticism or review, as permitted under the Copyright, Designs and Patents Act, 1988, no part of this publication may be reproduced, stored in a retrieval system, or transmitted in any form or by any means, electronic, electrical, chemical, mechanical, optical, photocopying, recording or otherwise, without the prior written permission of the copyright owner. Enquiries should be addressed to the Publishers.

Every attempt has been made by the Publishers to secure the appropriate permissions for materials reproduced in this book. If there has been any oversight we will be happy to rectify the situation and a written submission should be made to the Publishers.

A CIP catalogue record for this book is available from the British Library.

Shire Library no. 611   ISBN-13: 978 0 74780 810 7

Sally Badham has asserted her right under the Copyright, Designs and Patents Act, 1988, to be identified as the author of this book.

Designed by Tony Truscott Designs, Sussex, UK
Typeset in Perpetua and Gill Sans.
Printed and bound in Great Britain.

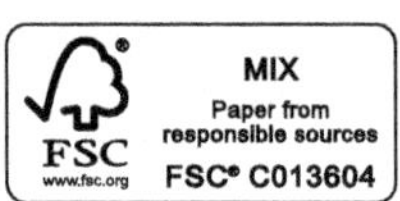

COVER IMAGE
Cover design and photography by Peter Ashley. Front cover: Detail of Stafford tomb chest in St. Peter's, Lowick, Northamptonshire. Back cover: detail from The Alabaster Lady tomb in Melton Mowbray parish church, Leicestershire.

TITLE PAGE IMAGE
Ewelme (Oxfordshire): Alice de la Pole, Duchess of Suffolk (died 1475). See also page 8 and the text on page 16.

CONTENTS PAGE IMAGE
Southover (East Sussex): Gundrada (died 1085), wife of William de Warenne, the founder of Lewes Priory.

DEDICATION
For my husband, Tim, and my close friends Moira and Brian Gittos, with whom in the course of several decades I have visited many churches in search of monuments. This book would have been the poorer without their willingness to share their knowledge and expertise.

ACKNOWLEDGEMENTS
I am grateful to the following for help with the text: Jerome Bertram, Philip Lankester, Sophie Oosterwijk, Nigel Saul and Christian Steer. Patrick Farman and Peter Hacker have helped to compile the gazetteer. For illustrations, I am grateful to Jon Bayliss, John Crook, Brian and Moira Gittos, David Griffith, Julian Luxford, Sophie Oosterwijk, Roger Rosewell, Martin Stuchfield, Kelcey Wilson-Lee, and, above all, Cameron Newham.

Illustrations are acknowledged as follows:

Sally Badham, pages 12 (top left), 17 (bottom); 29, 30 (bottom), 34 (top), 40 (bottom), 41, 56 (top); Jon Bayliss, page 12 (bottom); John Crook, pages 7 (top), 14 (left), 15 (left), 53 (top left), 62; Brian and Moira Gittos, pages 7 (bottom), 21 (bottom), 34 (bottom); 45 (top right); 46 (top left); F. A. Greenhill (rubbing), pages 28 (right), 39 (top); David Griffith, pages 16 (bottom), 28 (left), 35; Julian Luxford, page 32; Sophie Oosterwijk, page 51 (top); Roger Rosewell, page 17 (bottom); Les Smith, page 48; Martin Stuchfield, pages 13, 25 (top), 46 (top right); Kelcey Wilson-Lee, pages 18 (top), 22 (top), and 23.

The remaining images, including the cover, title page and contents page, are courtesy of C. B. Newham.

Shire Publications is supporting the Woodland Trust, the UK's leading woodland conservation charity, by funding the dedication of trees.

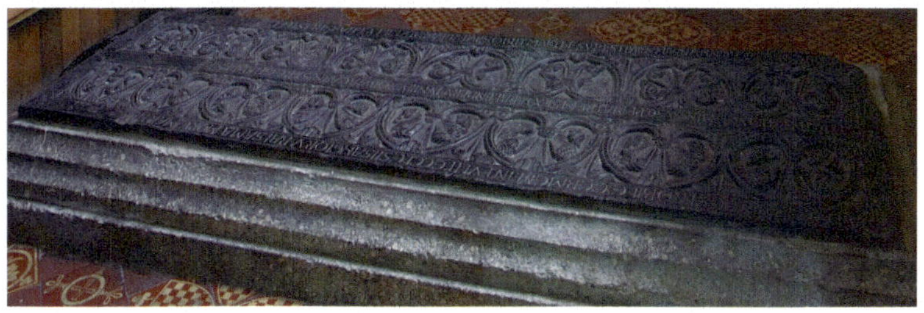

CONTENTS

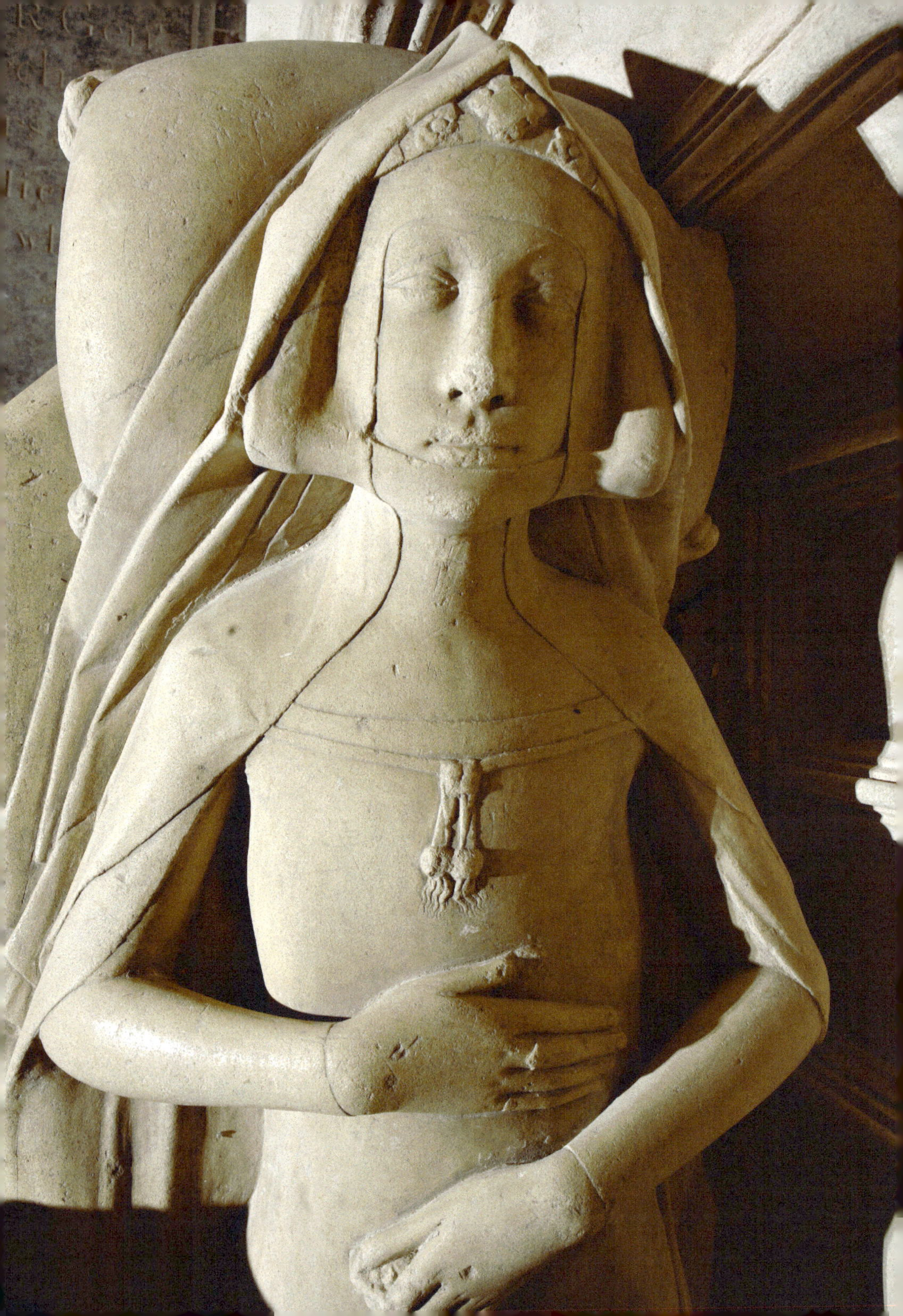

WHY STUDY CHURCH MONUMENTS?

CHURCHES contain much of the most interesting medieval sculpture in Britain. The finest church monuments, if in an art gallery, well-lit and with explanatory notices, would be nationally known and fêted. The magnificent gilded cast copper-alloy effigy from St Mary, Warwick, of Richard Beauchamp, Earl of Warwick (died 1439), with its perfect representation of Milanese armour and the finely observed detail down to the veins in the back of his hands, provoked awe and wonder at the 'Gothic' exhibition in London in 2003. Stone effigies can be equally impressive, conjuring up glamorous images of the age of chivalry. Sir Oliver de Ingham (died 1349) at Ingham (Norfolk), who lies alert on a bed of stones, is the very image of Christian knighthood as described in the *Chanson de Roland*. While alive, the knight can never rest; he is always travelling over harsh terrain, ready to draw his sword at any moment in defence of the faith; his eyes are fixed on heaven, where he will eventually have his reward. At Much Marcle (Herefordshire), Blanche, Lady Grandison (died 1347), with her beautiful, serene face and her delicate hands holding a rosary, reminds us of the gentle, high-born lady for whose favours knights competed in medieval romances.

Yet in their intended setting such monuments are little known to non-specialists. One of the joys of visiting churches is the experience of lighting upon these sculptural treasures. Not all are of a high standard, some being vernacular in character, but they illustrate the skills of medieval designers and sculptors. They open doors into the past and introduce us to characters from our history books who inhabited that lost world. Their designs can tell us much about the self-image of those commemorated and how they wanted to be remembered.

Medieval tomb monuments range from humble cross-slabs, without inscriptions, commemorating people whose identity has long been forgotten, through floor slabs with incising or inlays and often with inscriptions, to large and elaborate sculpted memorials to the nobility, higher clergy and even royalty. Most are to be found inside churches and cathedrals, sometimes in

Opposite:
Much Marcle
(Herefordshire):
Blanche, Lady
Grandison (died
1347). Her figure
is carved with
exceptional
delicacy, especially
her fingers holding
a rosary.

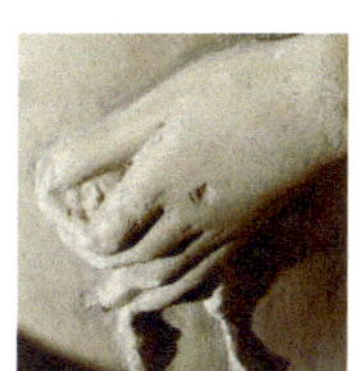

purpose-built chapels, although there remain a surprisingly large number of medieval churchyard monuments. Many monuments were probably set up soon after the person commemorated died, but some considered it wise to

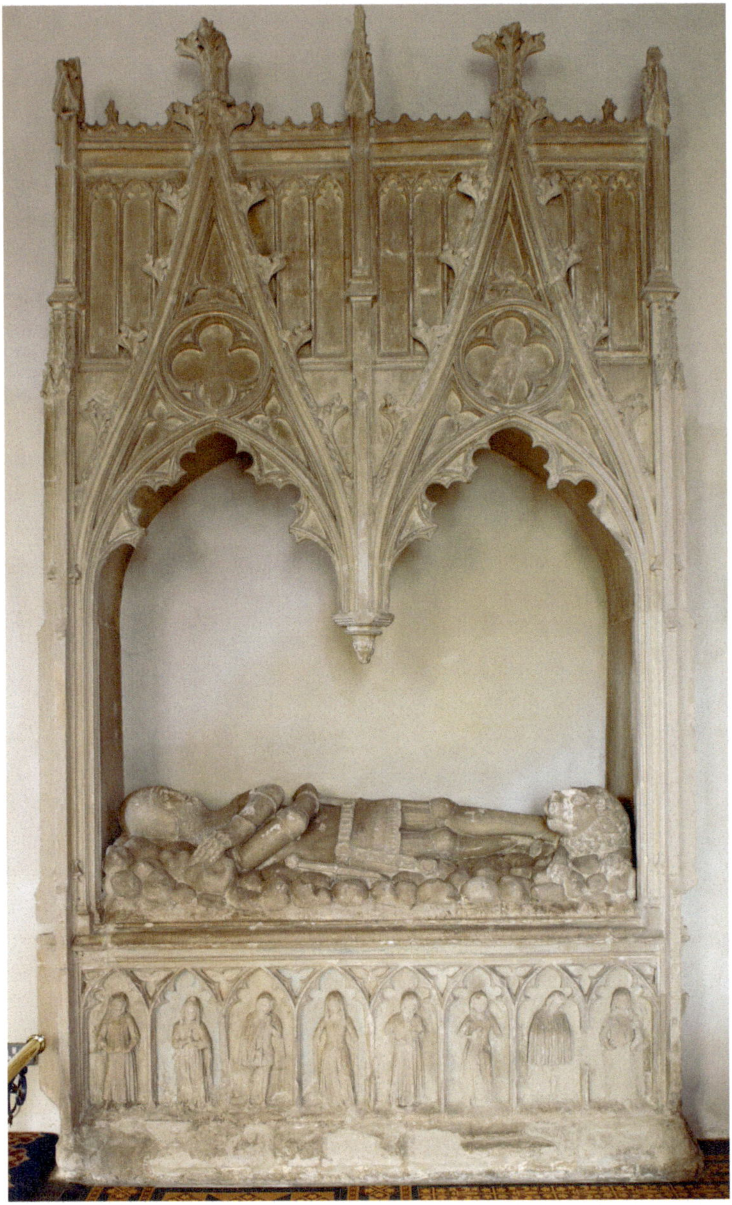

Right: Reepham (Norfolk): William de Kerdistan (died 1361). He lies under a fine canopy on a bed of stone on a tomb-chest with 'weepers' in the niches.

Below: Ingham (Norfolk): Sir Oliver de Ingham (died 1349). His effigy is the embodiment of Christian knighthood, always ready to act in defence of his faith.

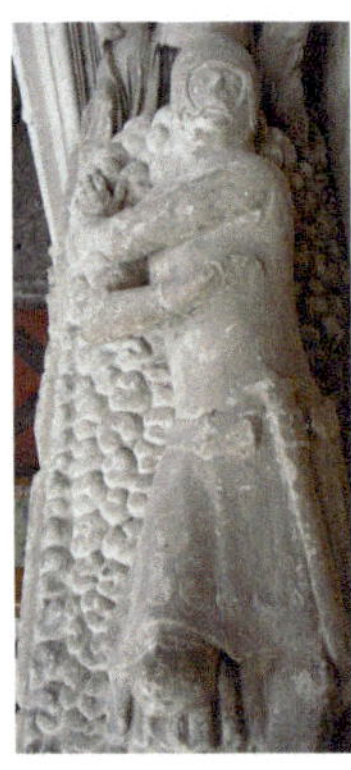

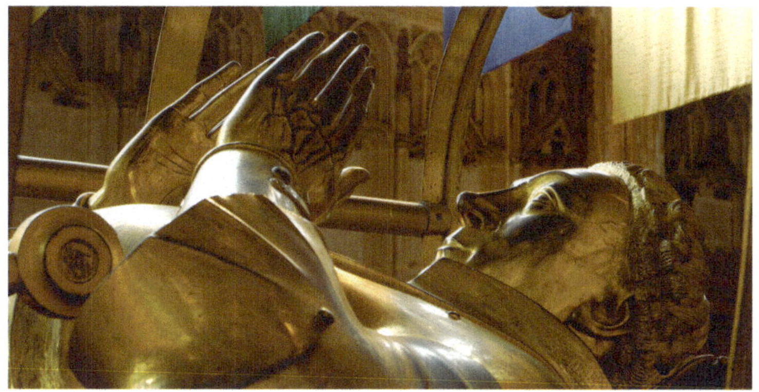

Warwick (Warwickshire): cast copper-alloy effigy of Richard Beauchamp, Earl of Warwick (died 1439). The monument cost £730, a huge sum for that date. The modelling is exceptionally lifelike.

act in their own lifetime. In Shakespeare's *Much Ado about Nothing*, Benedick observes: 'If a man do not erect in this age his own tomb ere he dies, he shall live no longer in monument than the bell rings, and the widow weeps.'

Some good books on medieval monumental sculpture were published in the early twentieth century, but the study of monuments other than brasses fell into the doldrums in the next fifty years. It was not until the Church Monuments Society was established in 1979, bringing together scholars, previously working in isolation, that interest in the subject was revitalised. Increasing awareness advanced our knowledge and led to new insights. It is now a multi-disciplinary study, carried out by art historians, archaeologists, historians, genealogists, students of costume, armour and heraldry, and by those who merely love churches and their contents.

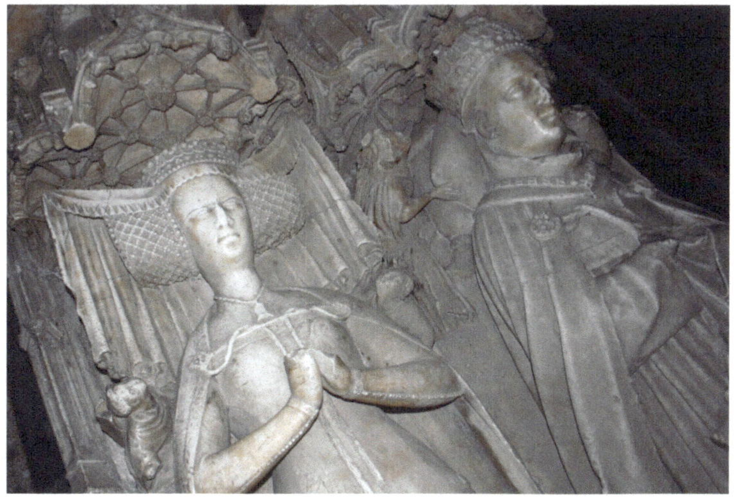

Arundel (West Sussex): Thomas Fitzalan, Earl of Arundel, and his wife, Beatrix (c. 1420). The use of alabaster enabled her elaborate horned headdress to be carved in fine detail.

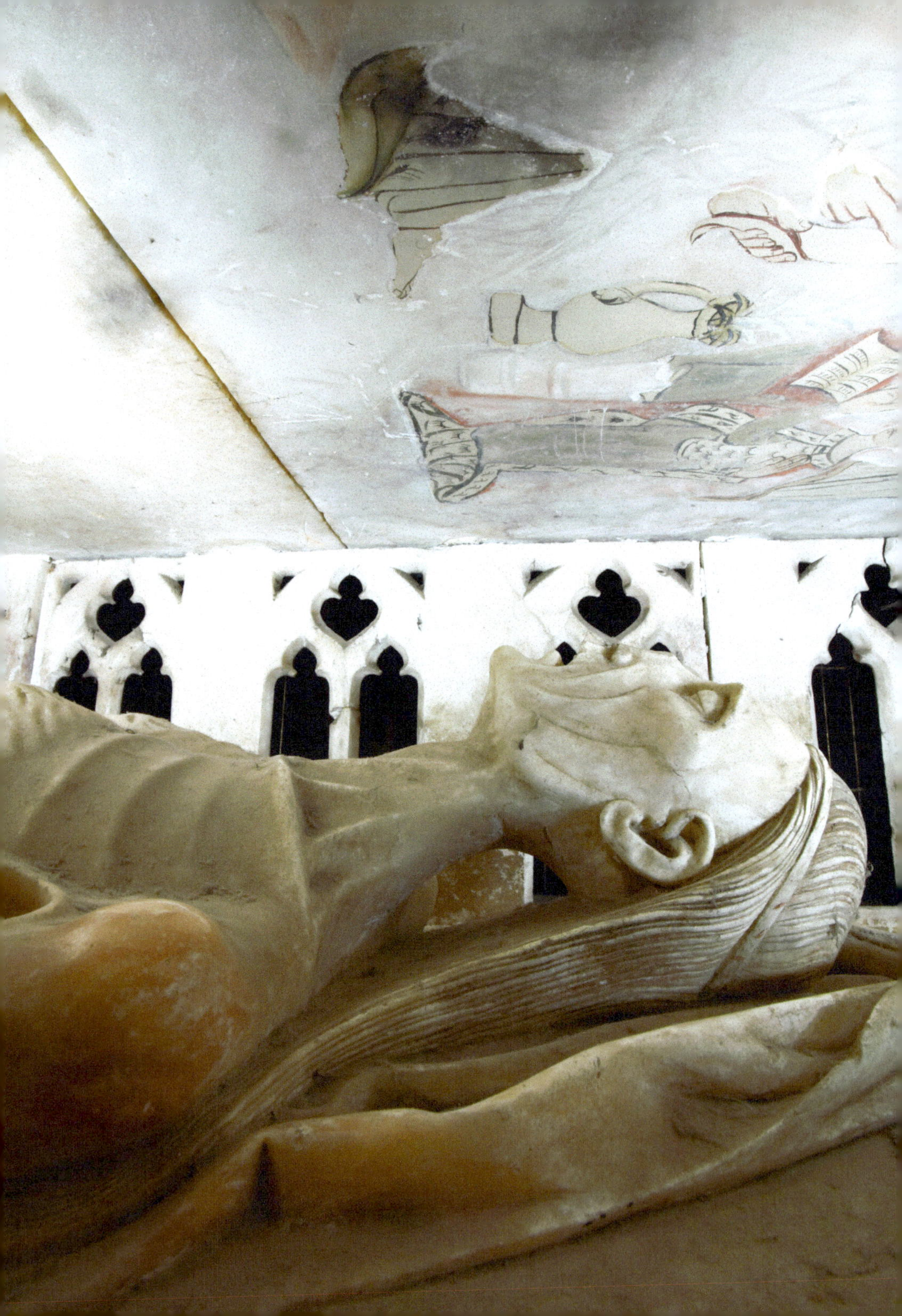

PURPOSE AND MEANING

Nowadays, when we plan tombstones for our loved ones, it is so that they will be remembered; the wording on the stone honours them as individuals or for their worldly achievements. These considerations were also important in the Middle Ages and are indeed often the most prominent aspects of medieval monuments. They helped to provide solace to grieving relatives and were crucial to the strategies by which families drew attention to their status and affirmed their position in society, whether they formed part of a noble or a mercantile elite.

For the nobility and gentry, family and lineage were central to their identity. They used heraldry not just for the purpose of enabling military identification, but to assert status and blood. A display of arms on their tombs encapsulated who they were and the distinguished families into which they and their ancestors had married. On some monuments heraldry is the main feature. There are many low-relief slabs in North Wales featuring a sword and shield, normally with the name of the commemorated, but those at Butterwick (North Yorkshire) and Salford (Bedfordshire) lack inscriptions. On the latter the sword could also be interpreted as a cross, possibly a deliberate ambiguity. Many thirteenth- and fourteenth-century monuments in particular no longer display inscriptions. They might have been just painted on, as on the back wall of the monument to Sir Henry Vernon (died 1514) at Tong (Shropshire), although some had separate parchment or wooden 'tables' that named the deceased. Those commemorated by now anonymous tombs can often be identified through the heraldry or the crests on helmets upon which some effigies rest their heads.

Until the mid-fourteenth century, those commemorated by effigies in armour bore their arms on their shield. When shields were no longer routinely carried, the arms were commonly shown on the coat armour that was worn on top of body defences of mail and plate. Arms were sometimes carved, but in many cases the heraldry was painted on and has since worn away, as is the case with a tomb featuring a military figure and lady at Winterbourne (Gloucestershire). Here there is no inscription naming the

Opposite:
Ewelme (Oxfordshire): Alice de la Pole, Duchess of Suffolk (died 1475). The cadaver on the lower layer of this 'double-decker' tomb gazes at painted imagery above. The effigy would also have been painted.

man commemorated, and his shield, which would have displayed his arms, has been almost completely broken away. The only clue to identity is that the knight rests his head on a helm surmounted by a crest of a boar's head, that of the Bradeston family, enabling the man commemorated to be identified as probably Thomas, Lord Bradeston (died 1360), a soldier and administrator whose service to the dominant Berkeley family transformed him from the obscure son of a minor landowner into a man of great power in Gloucestershire. In many cases, these identifiers enable us to link the material remains of the tomb monument with known historic facts about the lives of the commemorated, but not always. One of the most elaborate semi-effigial slabs – those on which the head and perhaps other parts of the body can be seen through shaped apertures – is that at Brize Norton

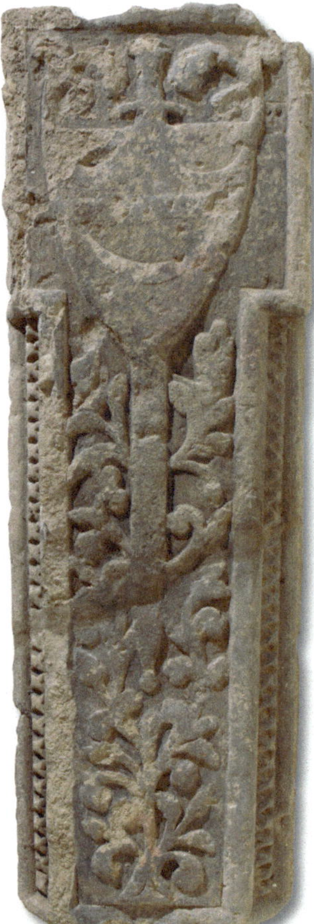

Right: Butterwick (North Yorkshire). The main features of this slab are a shield and a sword but the person commemorated has not been identified.

Far right: Brize Norton (Oxfordshire): Sir John Daubeney (died 1346). This fine example of a semi-effigial monument showing only part of the figure has an elaborate heraldic display.

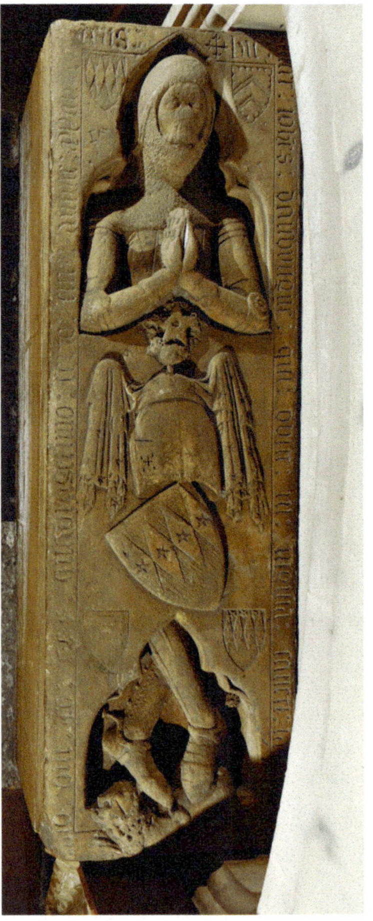

(Oxfordshire), which the inscription identifies as Sir John Daubeney (died 1346), of whom nothing can be traced in the written records.

Heraldry was not confined to the monuments of men. Ladies were equally keen to show their lineage through heraldry, displayed in a variety of ways. The effigy at Abergavenny Priory (Monmouthshire) of Eva, daughter and heiress of William de Braose, Lord of Abergavenny (died 1246), shows her with a large shield on her breast with the arms of her husband, William (III) de Cantilupe. The Frosterley marble effigy at Easington (County Durham) probably commemorating Isabella Bruce, the illegitimate daughter of William the Lion, king of Scotland, can be identified as the first wife of John FitzMarmaduke (died *c.* 1285) by the FitzMarmaduke popinjays carved on her supertunic. The lady at Much Marcle (Herefordshire) is identified as Blanche, Lady Mortimer (died 1347), wife of Sir Peter Grandison, through the heraldry positioned more conventionally on her tomb-chest and canopy. Some heiresses, conscious that their parentage was superior to that of their husbands, chose to prioritise their natal arms. The will of Margaret Paston (died 1484), heiress of the Mautbys and a familiar personality in the Paston Letters, gave instructions as to the form of her brass, which was to have a proud display of Mautby-related heraldry, with only one shield including her husband's arms.

Those of lesser rank were also eager to ensure that their monuments reflected their status. Some, such as clerics, lawyers and academics, were shown in the special garments of their profession, as were civic dignitaries. The mercantile equivalent of heraldry was the merchant's mark, which they would have used to mark their goods and which would have been immediately recognisable to their peers. Probably the earliest representation of such a mark on a monument in England occurs on an incised slab at Wyberton (Lincolnshire), imported from the Low Countries, which commemorates Adam de Franton (died 1325) and his wife, Sibile. By the fifteenth century merchants' marks were commonplace on incised slabs and brasses. They are rarer on high tombs, but the canopy of the tomb to William Canynges (died 1474) in St Mary Redcliffe, Bristol, has an angel with a shield

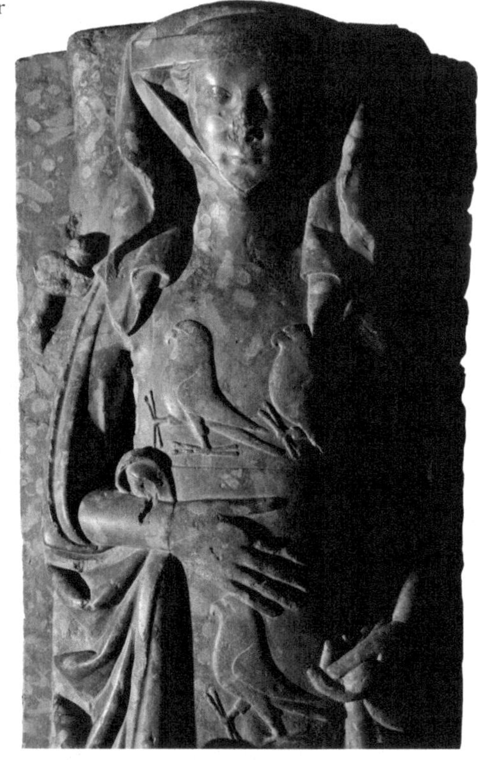

Easington (County Durham): Isabella Bruce, illegitimate daughter of William the Lion, king of Scotland, and wife of John FitzMarmaduke (died c. 1285). It is carved from Frosterley marble.

Right: Wadworth (South Yorkshire). The figure is shown wearing a *collobium* and cassock (legal dress) and so may commemorate the lawyer Sir John de Doncaster (died after 1334).

Far right: Harewood (West Yorkshire): Sir William Gascoigne, Lord Chief Justice (died 1419). He is shown in legal robes.

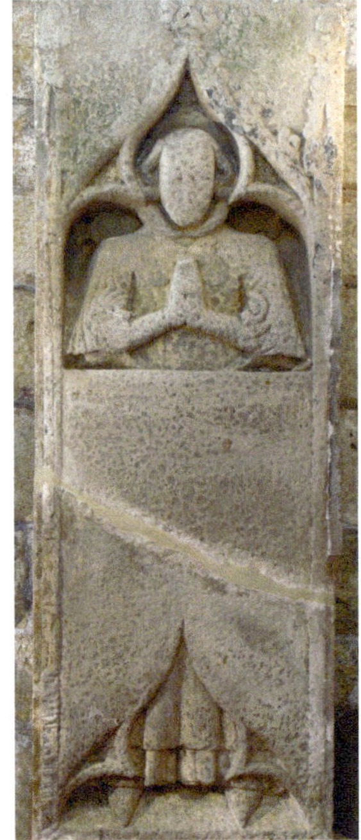

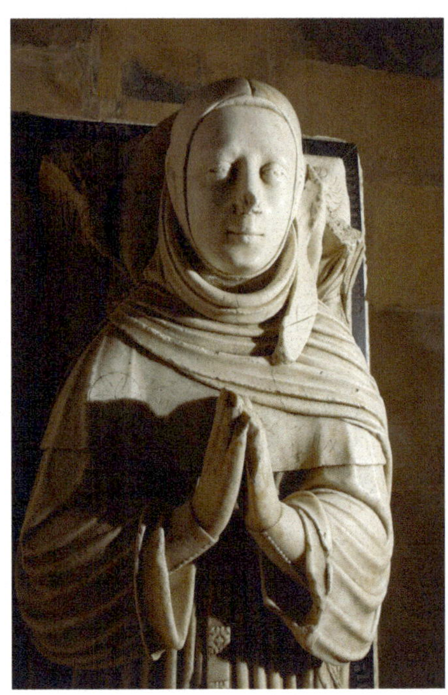

St Thomas, Salisbury (Wiltshire): Purbeck marble tomb-chest to an unknown merchant, showing his merchant's mark in the central shield.

bearing his mark; a Purbeck marble tomb-chest in St Thomas, Salisbury, has a merchant's mark in a shield in the middle of its long side; and an effigy of an unknown merchant recut to form part of a tomb canopy, now displayed in the café area of Exeter Cathedral (Devon), has his mark on a woolsack at his feet.

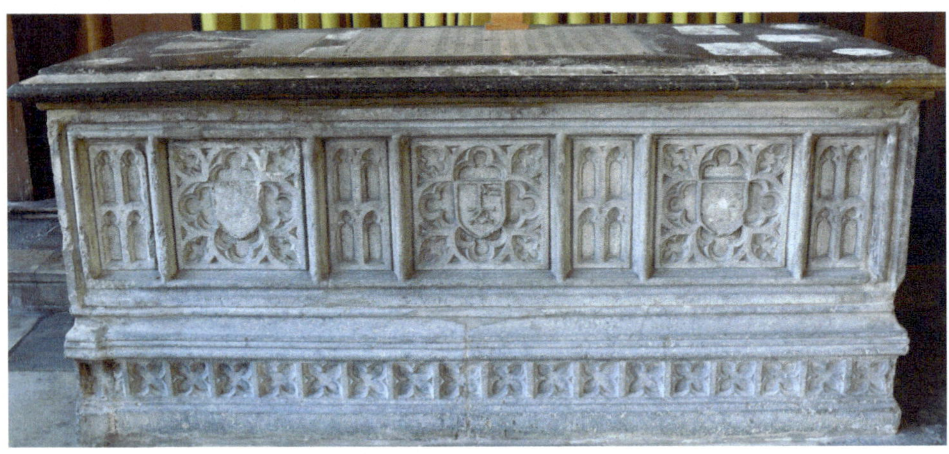

Merchants' marks were supplemented by other indicators of profession. Wool merchants are commonly shown with woolsacks or sheep as footrests. In the crypt of Hereford Cathedral is an alabaster incised slab commemorating Andrew Jonis (died 1497); the inscription tells us that he rebuilt the charnel house in the crypt and established a chantry there, but it is the cider barrel beneath his feet that indicates his trade.

Yet merchants' marks were not the earliest marks of status to appear on monuments. In the north, in particular, many cross-slabs carry secondary emblems to indicate the status of the deceased. Some are gender-specific, such as the sword for a man – with a possible additional meaning that the person commemorated was of at least gentry status – and the shears for a woman. Others indicate profession, such as the chalice, paten and book for a priest. All these priestly symbols can be combined with the sword, as at Carlatton Farm (Cumbria) on a slab commemorating Henry de Newton (died 1344) – not to indicate the church militant but that the priest commemorated was of gentle blood. A fragment at Rothwell (West Yorkshire) has a pair of horseshoes, perhaps for a blacksmith, while foresters may be indicated by a bow, as at Westerdale (North Yorkshire) and Wentworth (South Yorkshire), or a horn, as at St Oswald, Durham city. Cross-slabs in Cumbria at Lanercost Priory and St Bees are of great interest in that they show the pilgrim's scrip or purse.

These and other symbols of identity were also used on other monumental types. A semi-effigial monument at South Cave (Yorkshire East Riding) has as identifiers a shield, the initials 'IB' and a mason's square; it commemorates John Barton, mason, who willed to be buried in the church in 1483. In Lincolnshire, incised slabs to masons or architects are to be found in Lincoln Cathedral, to Richard de Gaynisburgh (c.1340), believed to have been the architect of the Angel Choir, and at Croyland Abbey to William de Wermington (c.1330). Effigies to foresters, shown carrying a hunting horn, can be found at Wadworth (South Yorkshire) and Skegby (Nottinghamshire).

Clerical effigies are obvious from their attire but often also display symbols of their calling, notably chalices and croziers;

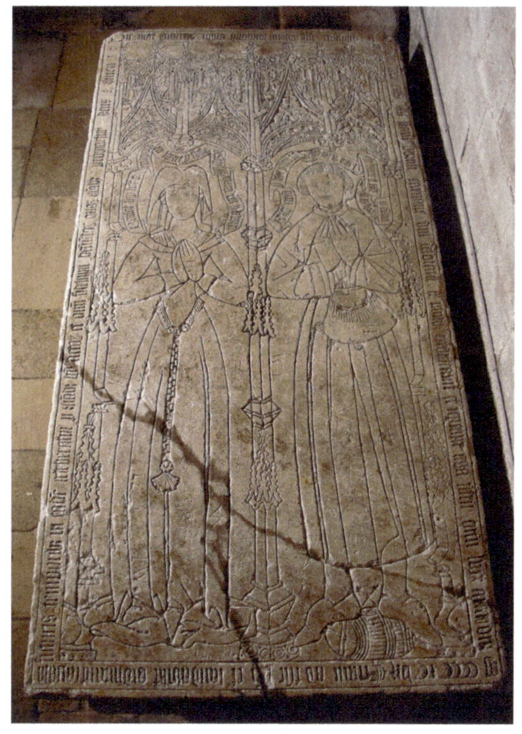

Hereford Cathedral crypt: Andrew Jonis (died 1497). A fine alabaster incised slab showing him with a cider barrel at his feet.

burials of clerics often include these items, although grave goods were otherwise uncommon in the later Middle Ages. From the twelfth century bishops and abbots were often shown holding a crozier in their left hand and with the right hand raised in blessing; this pose was probably copied from their seals. A fine effigy in Tournai marble at Salisbury Cathedral (Wiltshire) is a retrospective commemoration of Bishop Roger (died 1139), probably carved in the 1170s. Other examples show the hands clasped in prayer, but with the crozier tucked into the crook of the arm, as with the effigy at Winchester Cathedral (Hampshire) to Bishop William of Waynflete (died 1486), Lord Chancellor of England. He was one of the greatest educational benefactors of late-medieval England, being the founder of Magdalen College and Magdalen College School, Oxford. Effigial monuments to lesser orders and to the parish clergy also included emblems of their calling. An effigy to an unknown priest at Geddington (Northamptonshire) shows him holding a chalice in one hand and a book in the other. At Rippingale (Lincolnshire) a deacon holds an open book; the pages are faintly carved with text seeking prayers for the soul of the commemorated man, Hugh, the son of John Goboad.

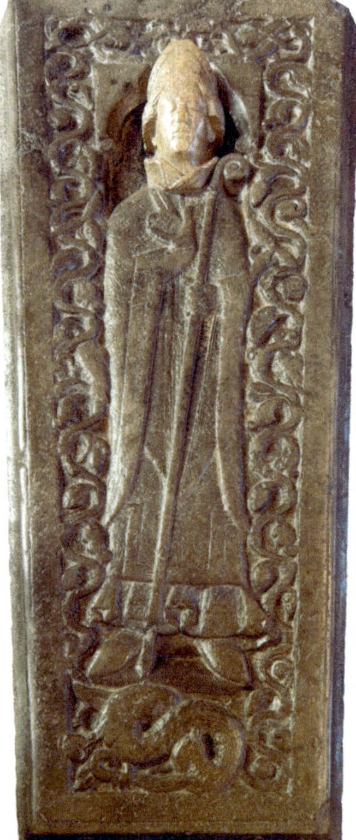

Right: Salisbury Cathedral (Wiltshire): Bishop Roger (died 1139). An early clerical effigy carved from Tournai marble.

Far right: Middleham (North Yorkshire): an emblematic slab to Robert Thornton, Abbot of Jervaulx (died 1510). His initials are shown on a tun.

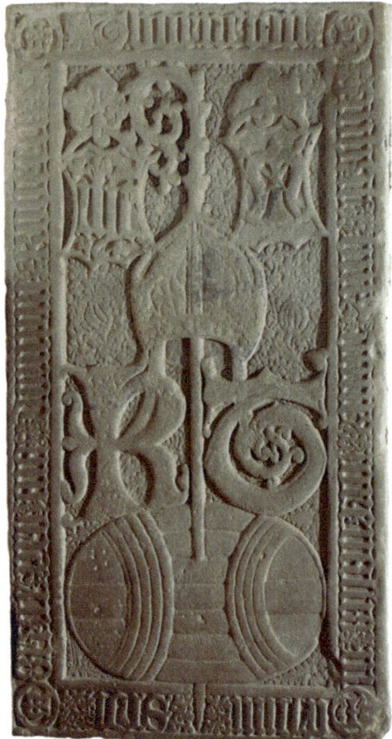

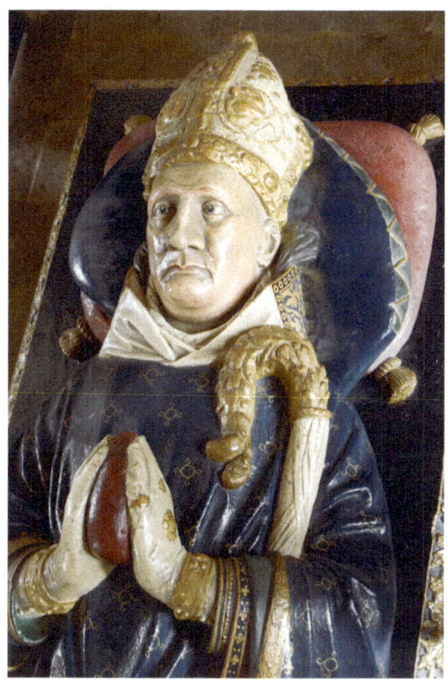

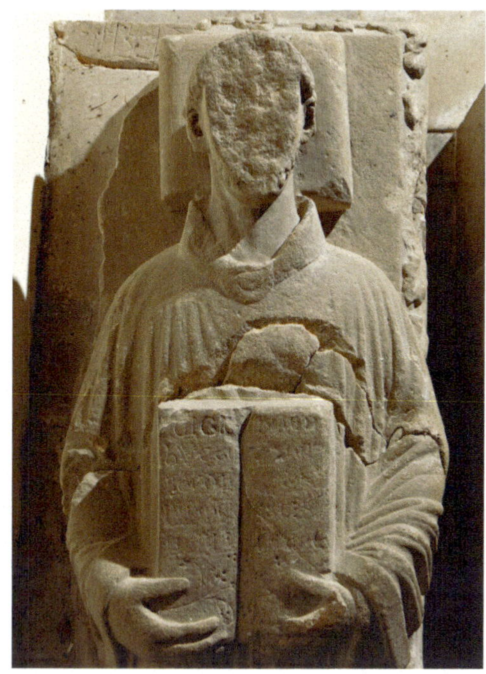

This takes us neatly to the primary purpose of monuments. In the Middle Ages the setting up of monuments was prompted not so much by the affairs of this world as by those of the world to come. Monuments had their setting in the context of medieval Catholic theology, specifically the doctrine of Purgatory, which held that the soul had to be refined or purified before it could enter heaven. Medieval man believed that the refining process could be speeded by the offer of prayers by the living faithful. The purpose of commissioning monuments was to enlist prayerful assistance from clergy, friends and onlookers. Thus the will of Robert Toste (died 1458), provost of the collegiate church of Wingham (Kent), requested 'a marble stone be laid over me with an inscription to induce people to pray for my soul'. If those who visited tombs could offer prayers for the deceased, the latter's soul would benefit. Monuments were thus a vital weapon in the battle for salvation of the soul.

Imagery reflecting prayer, intercession and salvation can be found on many tombs. Most effigies are shown with the hands together in prayer, as an exemplar to onlookers. The early-fourteenth-century lady at Axminster (Devon) is shown with a tiny image of the Virgin and Child within her hands, indicating the object of personal intercessory prayers. Sometimes the tomb-chest is populated by 'weepers' – figures, often depicted praying, which represent relatives or

Above left: Winchester Cathedral (Hampshire): Bishop William of Waynflete (died 1486). The effigy has been repainted to give an impression of the original appearance. The heart between his hands symbolises faith.

Above: Rippingale (Lincolnshire): a deacon holds an open book with a prayer for the soul of the commemorated, Hugh, the son of John Goboad.

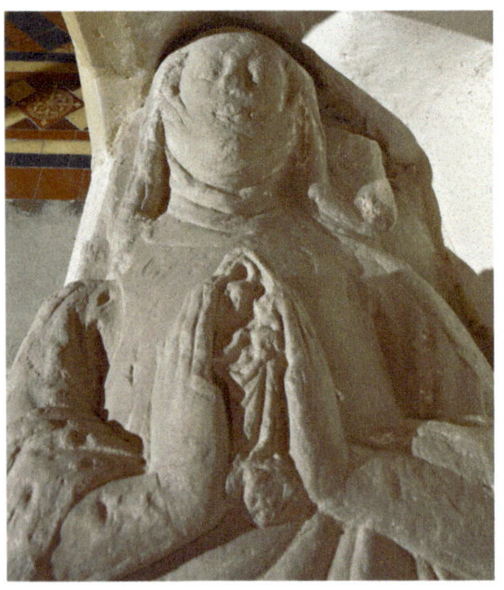

Axminster (Devon): an unknown lady of the early fourteenth century is shown holding a tiny image of the Virgin and Child.

associates of the deceased. Where the effigy is found in a chantry chapel, these figures with their associated identifying heraldry may have acted as an *aide-mémoire* for the priest, reminding him who should be named in the masses held daily for the commemorated and other beneficiaries. Examples include the monuments in Westminster Abbey to Edmund Crouchback, Earl of Lancaster (died 1296), Aymer de Valence, Earl of Pembroke (died 1324) and at Stanford-on-Teme (Worcestershire) to Sir Humphrey Salway (died 1493).

The prayers of the deceased and their kin or associates would sometimes be addressed to a specific saint. At Maidstone (Kent) the tomb with lost brass inlay to John Wootton (died 1417), first master of the collegiate church, has well-preserved remains of paintings showing him praying to an image of the Annunciation of the Blessed Virgin Mary, flanked by other saints. The effigy of an unknown priest at St David's (Pembrokeshire) has above his head a painted image of the Crucifixion, which reminds us of resurrection and salvation. Even more direct is the relationship shown at Ewelme (Oxfordshire) on the tomb to Alice de la Pole, Duchess of Suffolk (died 1475). This is a 'double-decker tomb' with an image of Alice in life above an effigy of her in death. Her gaunt and naked cadaver stares directly at an image of the Annunciation, while above her feet are images of Saints John the Baptist and Mary Magdalene (see page 8).

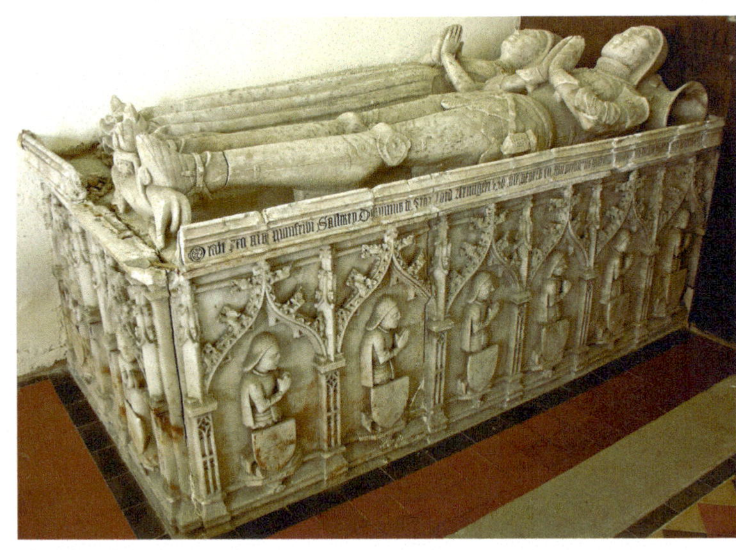

Stanford-on-Teme (Worcestershire): Sir Humphrey Salway (died 1493) and wife. The alabaster tomb-chest has kneeling figures; their shields would have been painted with their arms to identify them.

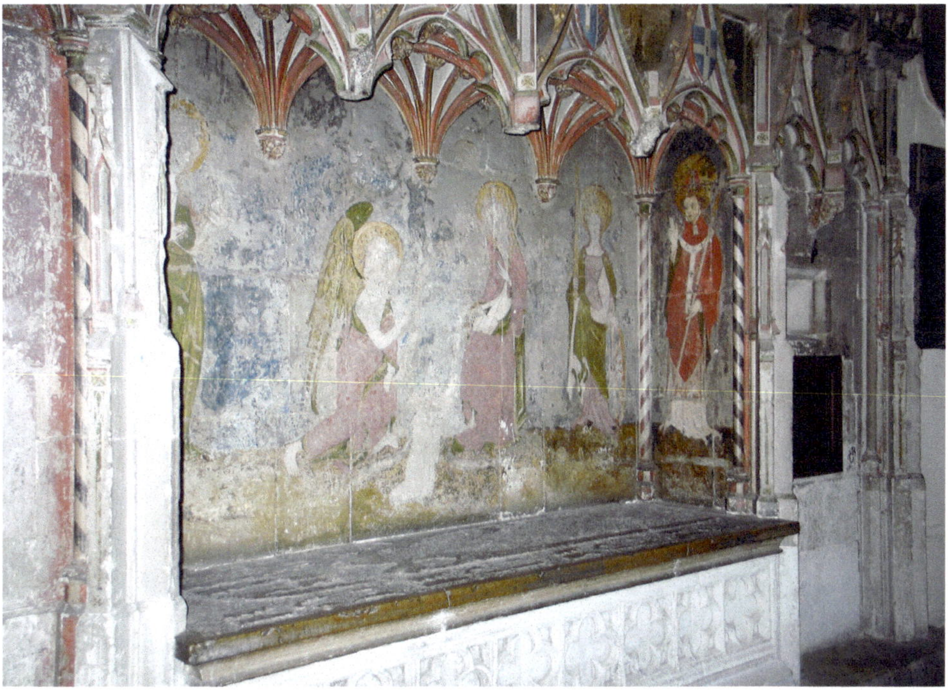

Images of salvation in the form of angels carrying the soul to heaven are more common, although they can be hidden among other carving, as on the gablette of a tomb to an unknown lady at Ropsley (Lincolnshire). An early example at Ely Cathedral (Cambridgeshire) probably commemorates Bishop Nigel (died 1163); here the image of the archangel Michael carrying the soul is the main feature of a Tournai marble tomb slab. They are shown under a canopy topped by buildings, perhaps representing the heavenly Jerusalem; similar canopies can be found at Avon Dassett (Warwickshire) on a monument to a deacon, probably Hugh (died *c.*1240), and at Peterborough Cathedral on some of the retrospective effigies to abbots carved from Alwalton marble. At Bakewell (Derbyshire) Sir Godfrey Foljambe (died 1376) and his wife are shown emerging from clouds, presumably in heaven.

All Saints church, Maidstone (Kent): the tomb, with lost brass inlay, to John Wootton (died 1417) has a painting of him as a small figure dressed in white, kneeling before the Annunciation of the Blessed Virgin Mary.

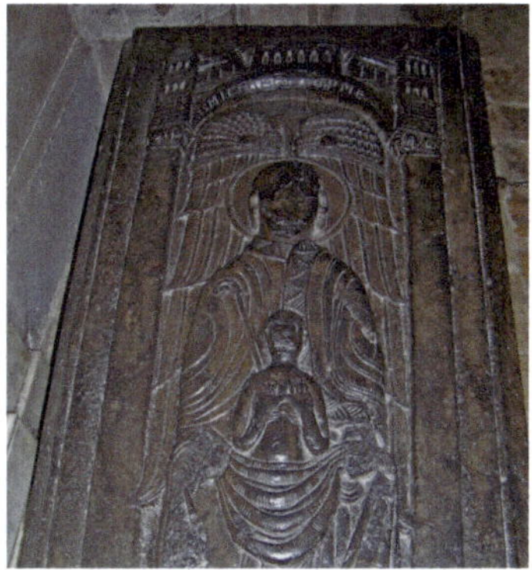

Ely Cathedral (Cambridgeshire): Bishop Nigel (died 1163). A figure representing his soul is held in a napkin by the archangel Michael.

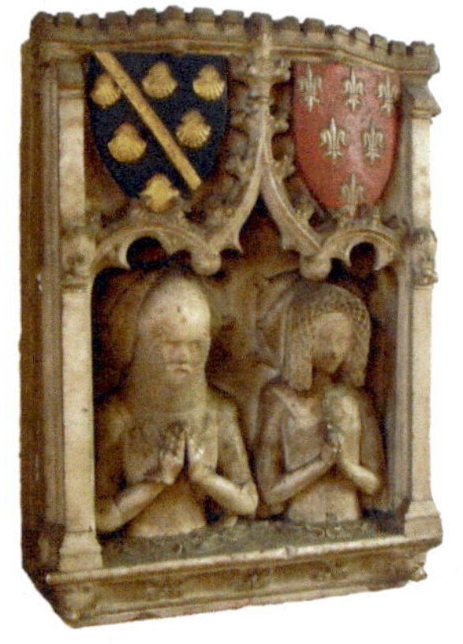

Bakewell (Derbyshire): Sir Godfrey Foljambe (died 1376) and his wife are shown emerging from clouds, presumably resurrected and in heaven.

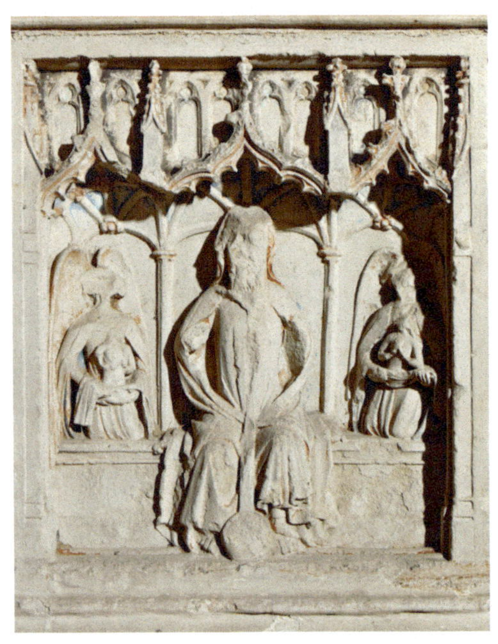

Ingham (Norfolk): Sir Roger de Boys (died after 1395) and his wife, Margaret. On the tomb-chest their souls are presented to the Trinity.

At Llandaff Cathedral (Cardiff) the monument to Bishop John Marshall (died 1496) incorporates a carved image of Jesus surrounded by symbols of his Passion, and has a tester – a wooden board hung over the effigy, now elsewhere in the cathedral – showing him venerating an image of the Assumption of the Virgin, while the retrospective tomb commemorating St Dyfryg has stone panels showing the Passion symbols and Christ rising from his tomb. On the monument to Sir Bartholomew Burghersh (died 1355) at Lincoln Cathedral a pair of angels carrying his soul are shown by his feet, balancing a pair of angels supporting his arms at his head. That to Sir Roger de Boys (died after 1395) and his wife at Ingham (Norfolk) has on the end panel of the chest an unusual representation of the souls being presented to the Trinity in a scene of the individual judgement; the choice is explained by the effigies being shown in the robes of the Guild of the Holy Trinity at Ingham, Roger being one of the founders. Many backs of tomb recesses, now entirely blank, probably originally held painted devotional imagery, long since flaked or cleaned off, but a soul-bearing angel survives inside the canopy on one of the tomb recesses at Winchelsea (Sussex).

Family members praying for the deceased could formerly be seen in association with other images of salvation and resurrection at Northmoor (Oxfordshire). The effigies of John de la More (died after 1361) and his wife, Isabel, were placed on tomb-chests – now lost – within a recess. The back wall of the recess and the area above it were painted with associated imagery, now mostly lost. Nearby is a better-preserved painting of Christ in Majesty. The whole scheme presents a narrative: the effigies indicate the death of the couple; the scene on the back wall of the recess shows them and their children praying for intercession; the image of Christ promises salvation; and the image of the soul-bearing angel above depicts the outcome of them being carried to heaven.

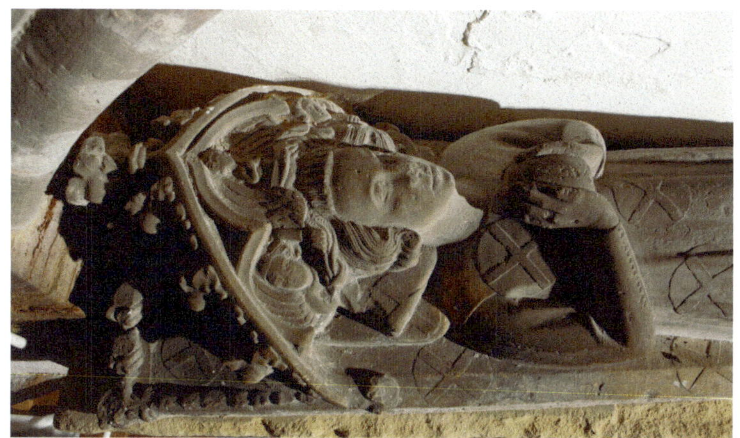

Left: West Leake (Nottinghamshire): an unknown civilian (*c.* 1320–30) with crosses on his gown, perhaps guild robes. In the canopy his soul is being carried to heaven.

Below: Northmoor (Oxfordshire): general view of fourteenth-century tombs to the de la More family with associated wall-paintings.

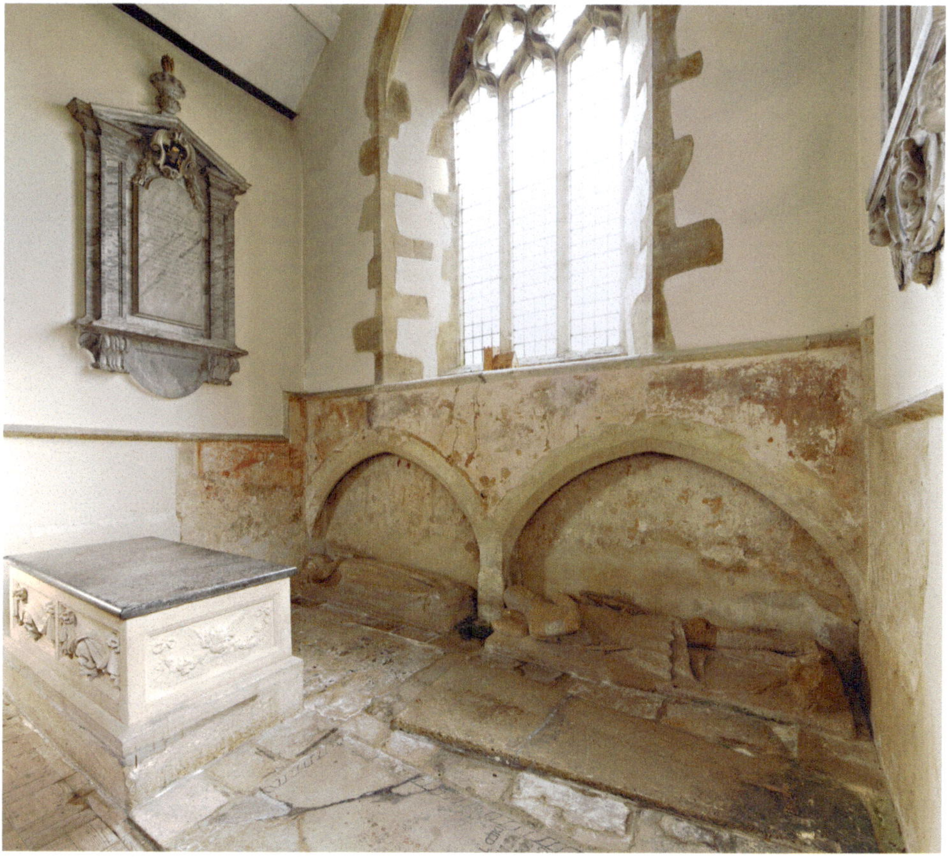

THE DEVELOPMENT OF CHURCHYARD MONUMENTS

MEDIEVAL CHURCHYARD monuments survive in far larger numbers than is normally credited. The earliest medieval Christian monuments in England and Wales were undoubtedly always intended to be located outside churches. Some early crosses were prominently placed in remote graveyards on hillsides but most pre-Conquest memorials covered churchyard graves. Their origins can be traced back to non-effigial types, often featuring interlace decoration, some of which date from the early Anglo-Saxon period. The extent to which Anglo-Scandinavian monuments in particular commemorate individuals rather than elite families or an entire community is debatable. A minority bear inscriptions, in runes, ogham or Roman script, identifying the commemorated, but prayers for the soul came later. A remarkable series, dating from the seventh to the ninth centuries, was excavated from a cemetery site beneath York Minster; they vary in quality, but most carry inscriptions suggesting production for a literate elite within the community.

From the ninth century, there was a rich tradition of commemorative sculpture, the main forms being raised crosses and long stones covering the graves flanked by upright head and foot stones. The most complete and elaborate surviving examples, albeit much later in date and several with effigial representation, comprise a group of six such grave markers in the cemetery of the remote ruined medieval church at Llanfihangel Abercywyn (Carmarthenshire). Other examples are at Meldon (Northumberland), Rodmell (Sussex) and Haresfield (Gloucestershire), demonstrating the wide spread of this form. A particularly attractive type of grave marker, limited to northern England and probably produced under Viking influence (although they do not appear in Scandinavia), is the hogback, an elaborately decorated, coped, house-shaped stone with bears clasped at each end. The largest series is to be found at Brompton-in-Allertonshire (North Yorkshire). Similar decorated coped stones, but lacking the bears, can be found in Cornwall, including at Lanivet and Phillack.

From the tenth and eleventh centuries, simple grave markers, normally marked with crosses, were produced in large numbers. Most often found,

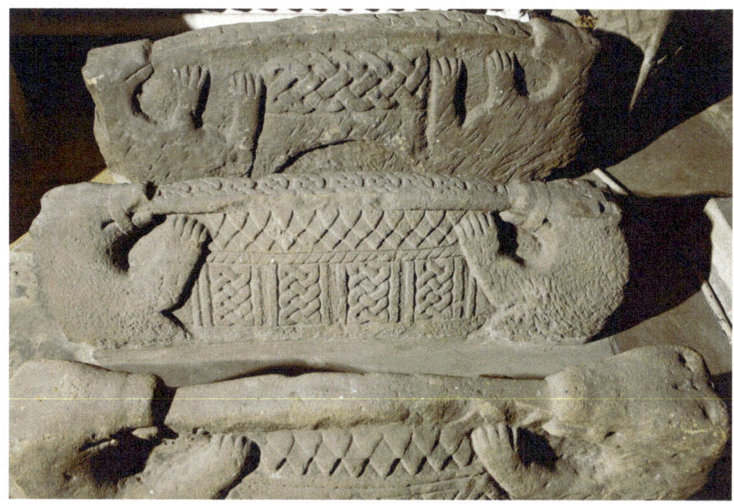

Brompton-in-Allertonshire (North Yorkshire): Anglo-Danish 'hogback' grave markers. These elaborately decorated, coped, house-shaped stones have bears clasped at each end.

in combination or separately, are full-length cross-slabs and discoid head and foot stones. A minority remain *in situ*; others have been moved and perhaps incorporated in the fabric of churches. Porches are often used to house displaced cross-slabs; large numbers are at Bakewell (Derbyshire) and Gainford (County Durham). Most cross-slabs are now removed from

Llanfihangel Abercywyn (Carmarthenshire): grave markers in the cemetery of the remote ruined medieval church. This assemblage is an exceptional survival.

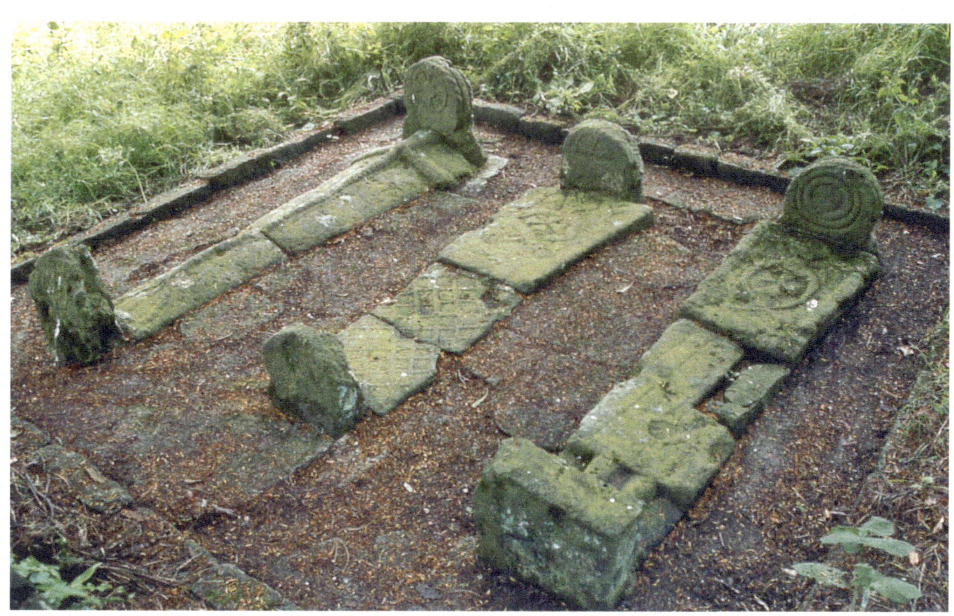

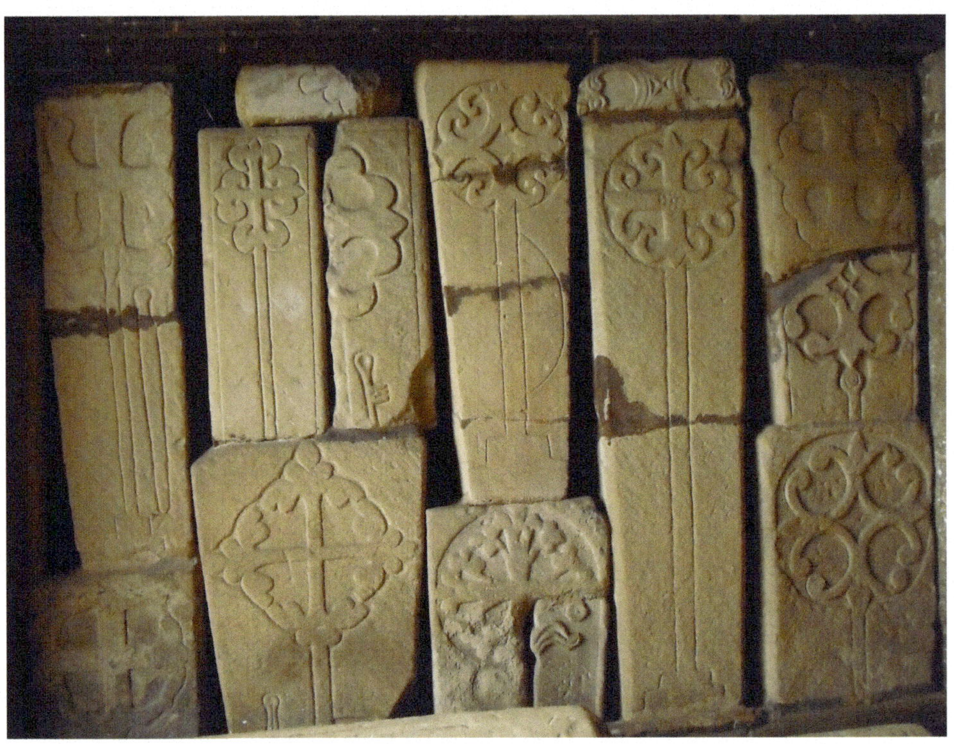

Bakewell (Derbyshire): some of the cross-slabs relocated in the porch.

Opposite top left: Welby (Lincolnshire): an early-fourteenth-century semi-effigial churchyard slab to an unknown lady and her child. Note the drainage holes.

their original context and instead built into walls, so it is not easy to establish whether many were intended as churchyard or church monuments. Some medieval grave markers have special characteristics; in the Cotswolds they tend to be coped, to help rain run off, and often have the gable ends marked by small carved crosses. Discoid head and foot stones were always intended purely as an external grave marker, but this type also has been recycled: one masquerades as a consecration cross at Steeple Barton (Oxfordshire).

In the later Middle Ages, almost every type of monument found within churches can also be found as a churchyard tomb, although not all monuments in churchyards were originally placed outside and some external monuments have been brought inside for better preservation. An early-fourteenth-century incised slab on a coffin at East Coker (Somerset) was excavated in the churchyard but may not have always been there. External brasses have also been recorded, for example at Westcot Barton (Oxfordshire). Semi-effigial monuments were one popular type, particularly in and near the Cotswolds. Collections of these and other recumbent churchyard monuments, almost certainly all *in situ*, are to be found at

Silchester (Hampshire) and Limpley Stoke (Wiltshire), although, being set directly into the ground, they have suffered greatly from exposure to the elements. A pair of semi-effigies on a tomb-chest at South Cerney (Gloucestershire) are better preserved, but possibly the finest example is the one now in the porch at Welby (Lincolnshire). This shows the bust of a lady in an aperture in the slab, beneath which is carved a blanket folded over at the top; below is carved a 'chrysom' infant. The slab may commemorate a woman who died in childbirth. The detail is so clear that it might be questioned whether it was ever outside, were it not for the tell-tale drainage holes in the aperture, which are a sure sign that the monument was intended to be outside.

Full-scale effigies were also carved for display in churchyards, although they tend to be simpler than interior effigies, with no undercutting or fine detail that might retain rainwater. An interesting group can be found at Leckhampton (Gloucestershire); the best preserved of these – to a priest – has been removed inside, with the remaining four – commemorating members of the laity – gathered together near the north porch, balancing a group of graveyard recumbent cross-slabs. Several of the effigies have a cross carved at the top end of the slab, as with Cotswold churchyard cross-slabs. At Tetbury (Gloucestershire) two churchyard effigies have been brought into the church. One to a civilian has prominent drainage holes and, at the top, a socket, which probably originally held an upright cross. A weathered churchyard effigy at Merthyr Mawr (Bridgend, Wales) has a curious protuberance at the top of the head, which might also have served as a fixing for a standing cross.

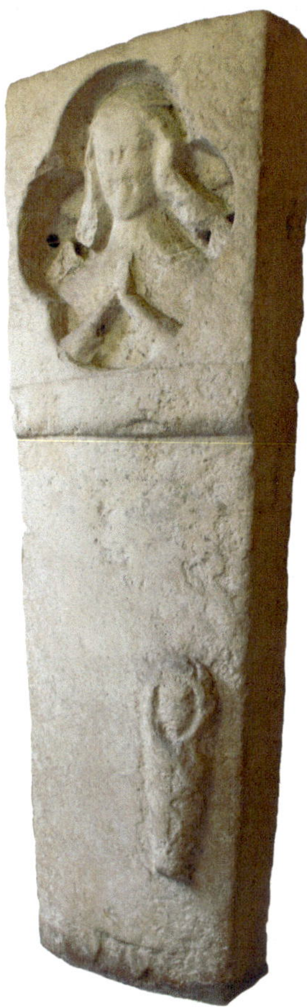
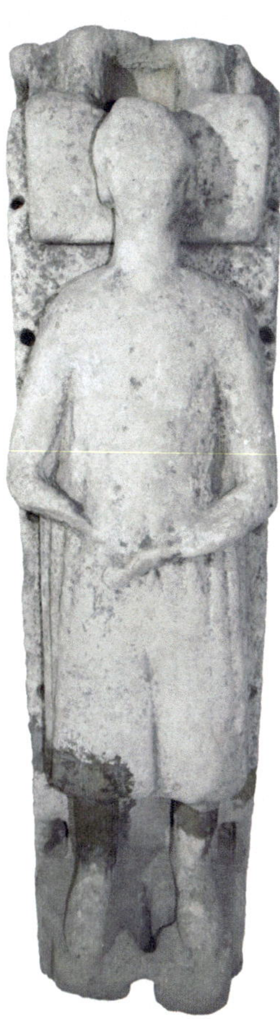

Above: Tetbury (Gloucestershire): mid-fourteenth-century churchyard effigy of an unknown civilian. It has prominent drainage holes and, at the top, a socket, which probably originally held an upright cross.

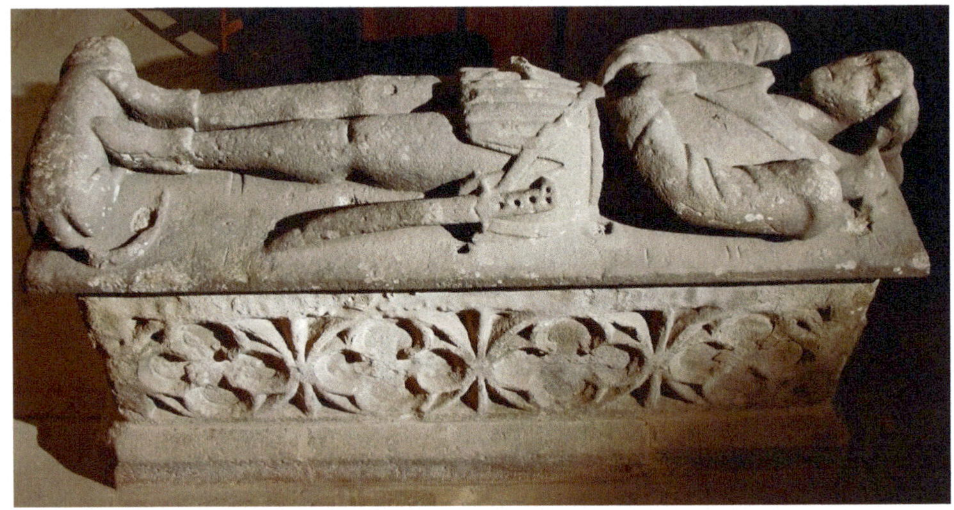

Above: Newland (Gloucestershire): Jenkin Wyrall, 'forester of fee' (died 1457). He sports a horn and dagger.

Opposite top: Loversall (South Yorkshire): early-fourteenth-century churchyard tomb-chest. It has a worn-relief cross-slab on the top but the main feature is the elaborate tracery on the sides.

Opposite bottom: Foulsham (Norfolk): Robart Colles (died after 1505) and his wife, Cecily; a churchyard tomb-chest with crowned letters spelling out the name of the person commemorated.

As with semi-effigial slabs, churchyard effigies survive in better condition when placed on tomb-chests, particularly if protected under an arched recess, as at Great Brington (Northamptonshire). The monument at Newland (Gloucestershire), now in the church, is a fine late example. An effigy of a man with a horn and dagger is displayed on an elaborately carved tomb-chest with an inscription identifying him as Jenkin Wyrall, 'forester of fee' (died 1457). It is exceptional to be able to put a name to the person commemorated by any medieval churchyard monument.

Churchyard tomb-chests are also worthy of study in their own right. Some regions have distinctive styles, the Cotswold chests being commonly decorated with a series of panels containing quatrefoils, as at Combe and Church Hanborough (Oxfordshire) and Buckland (Gloucestershire). A few are more elaborate, that at Fulbrook (Oxfordshire) having a Crucifixion on one end panel. Among the finest churchyard chests is the early-fourteenth-century example at Loversall (South Yorkshire) supporting a worn relief cross-slab, notable for the elaborate and varied tracery carved on its sides. At Bishops Cannings (Wiltshire) a chest features arcading with trefoiled heads; and at Foulsham (Norfolk) is a fine example with quatrefoils, mouchette wheels, diamonds and crowns, and an inscription to Robart Colles (died after 1505). It was probably originally inlaid with flush flintwork. The tomb-chest at Saxton (North Yorkshire) is plain apart from a shield of arms on each side, its importance being that it commemorates Ralph, Lord Dacre of Gilsland, who was killed at the Battle of Towton (1461), at which he commanded the left wing of the Lancastrian army. He was buried in an upright position, his horse under him.

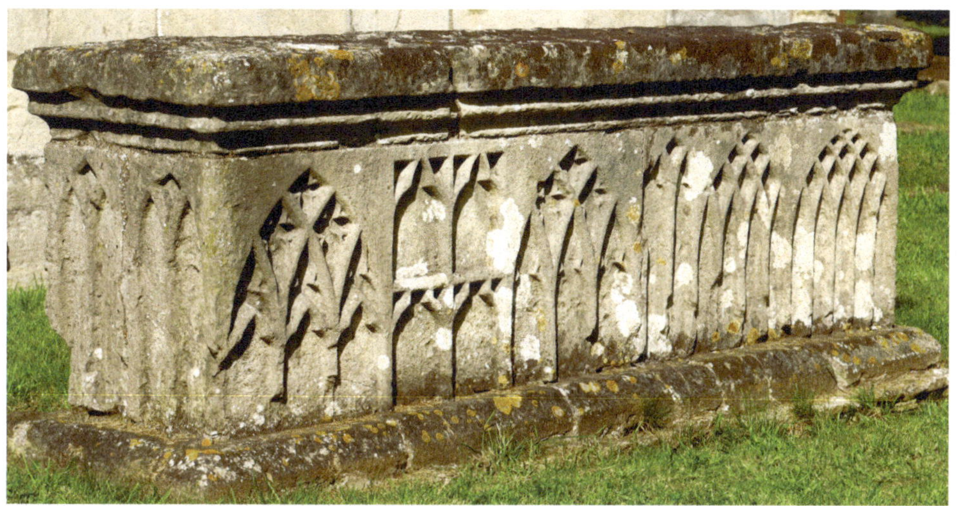

Some monuments were also mounted on the external walls of churches. A group of mural panels, carved in imported Caen stone and probably made in or near Chichester (West Sussex), around 1525–45, are characterised by dominant religious imagery, unusual in the opening years of the Reformation, and mix traditional Gothic motifs with the new Renaissance symbolism. Two are at St Andrew Oxmarket, Chichester, to Thomas Royse (*c.* 1525) and Willian Royse (*c.* 1540); both show a couple kneeling in prayer beneath images of saints. The same prolific workshop also produced monuments for inside churches, some of them very elaborate canopied affairs.

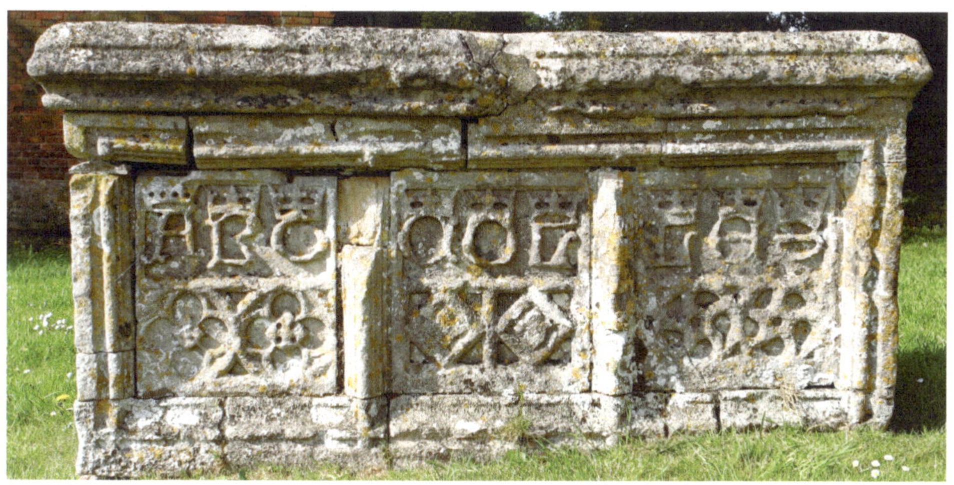

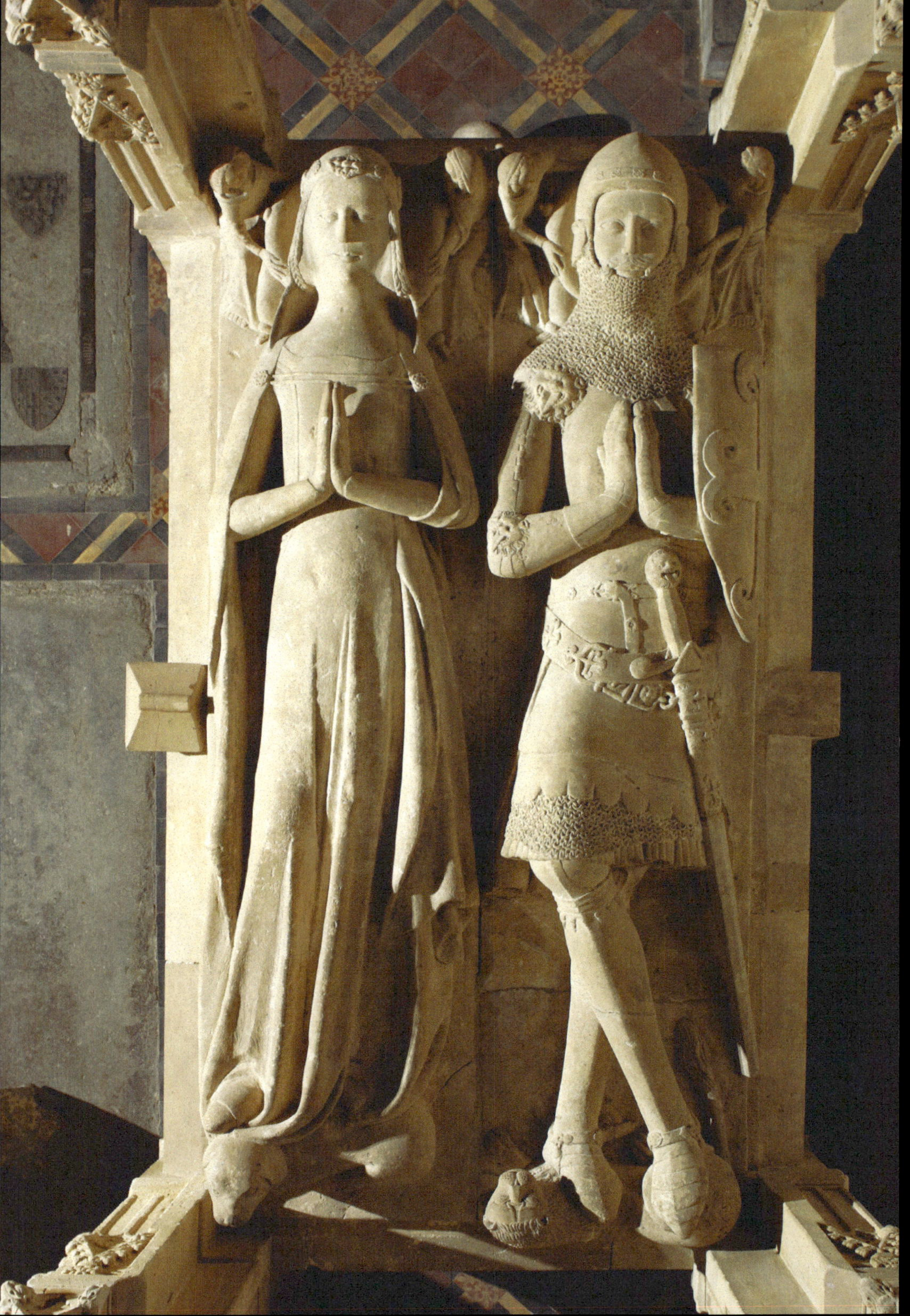

BURIAL AND COMMEMORATION INSIDE CHURCHES

Before the Norman Conquest most burials were in churchyards, but burial inside churches was permitted for the higher clergy, kings, princes and patrons following a decree of the Council of Mainz in 813. The extent to which this happened in England is difficult to establish. For some pre-Conquest burials there is documentary evidence, including the interment inside the church of St Olave, York, of its founder, Earl Siward (died 1055). Few monuments attributable to named individuals survive from that era, but post-Conquest examples include the inscription slab at Stratfield Mortimer (Berkshire) to Aethelweard, son of Cypping. Another, originally at Lewes Priory but now at Southover (East Sussex), commemorates Gundrada (died 1085), the wife of William de Warenne, Earl of Surrey, the priory's founder. It is unlikely that it was made immediately following her death, but it was probably commissioned by the monastic community in the twelfth century. That burial inside churches was becoming more widespread is clearly indicated by the survival in significant numbers, particularly in northern England, of tenth- and eleventh-century cross-slabs in parish churches in particular, where regulation may have been less rigorously enforced. Some may commemorate clerics, but many more probably marked the church burials of the local lay elite. Cross-slabs continued to be produced up to the Reformation.

Gradually the prohibition of non-clerical burials inside churches, particularly in monastic churches, was relaxed, as is demonstrated by successive Cistercian legislation. The first burial of lay founders within the confines of the monastery was permitted in 1157; by 1217 such founders and their descendants were allowed burial in cloister walks; from the mid-thirteenth century this was extended to the churches themselves; and by 1322 anyone who had contributed to the construction of the church could be buried within it.

Together with increased burial inside churches came greater formalisation of the doctrine of Purgatory, which placed more emphasis on the fate of the individual, rather than the Christian faithful as an entity.

Opposite:
Spilsby (Lincolnshire): John, second Lord Willoughby (died 1347), and his wife. This tomb has been restored, but remains an outstanding example of the main London workshop. The craftsmen evidently travelled to Lincolnshire to produce it as it is carved from local Ancaster limestone.

Right: Alvechurch (Worcestershire): Bishop Carpenter of Worcester (died 1476). The cross-slab has a chalice and his arms incorporating his mitre as identifiers.

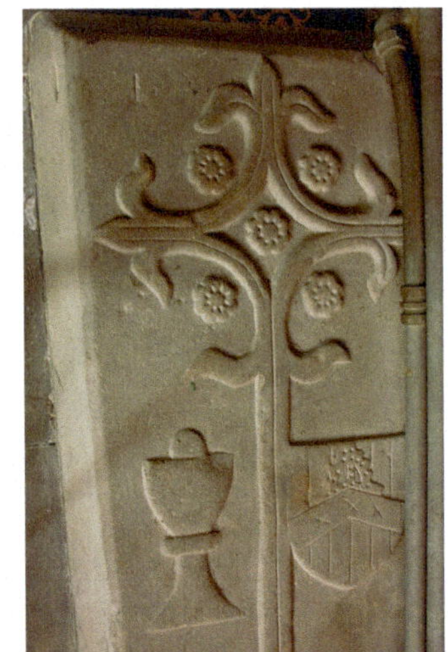

Far right: A rubbing from Sollers Hope (Herefordshire) of mid-thirteenth-century slab featuring a low-relief haloed cross-head above an incised effigy of a military figure in a pot helm.

Right: Bredon (Worcestershire): early-fourteenth-century semi-effigial monument to an unknown civilian and his wife. The Crucifixion imagery is a rare survival.

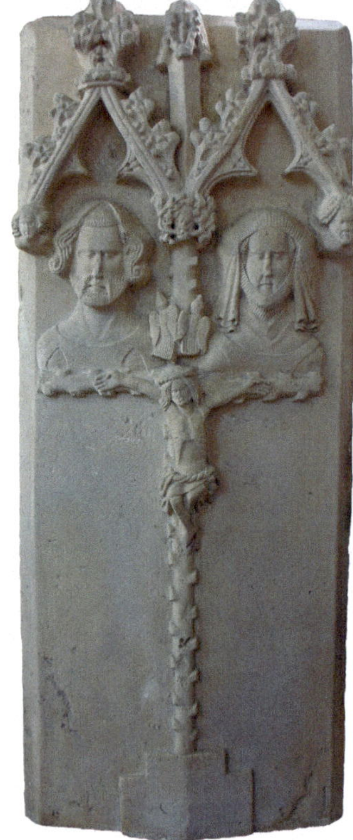

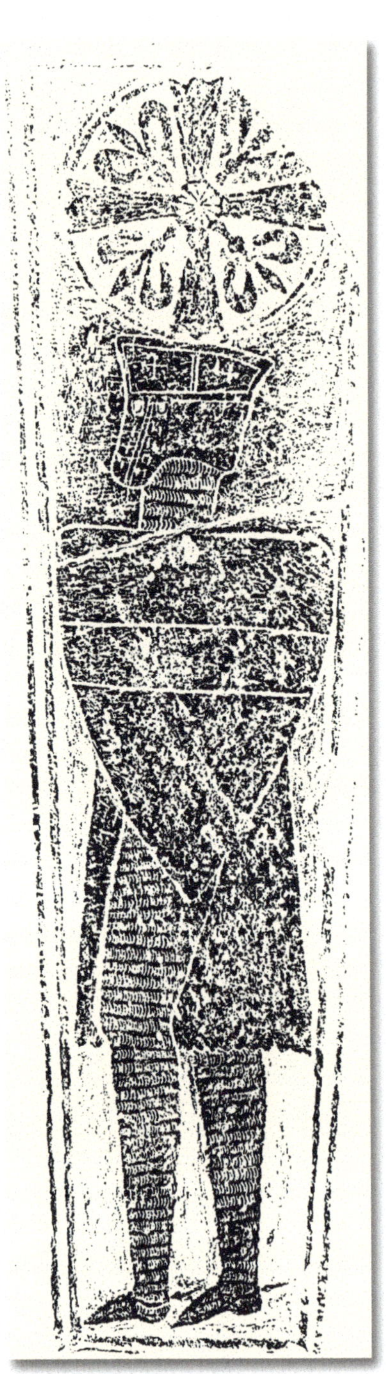

This spurred the development of monumental types with images of the deceased. Floor slabs diversified, with effigial representation supplementing or replacing the cross. An early example is a Purbeck marble slab of *c.* 1080–1130 from St Frideswide's Priory, Oxford, now in the Museum of Oxford; the top surface displays stylised crosses formed by groups of concentric semicircles with a rudimentary face at the centre. A mid-thirteenth-century slab at Sollers Hope (Herefordshire) shows a haloed cross-head with an incised effigy of a military figure in a pot helm below. The earliest effigial incised slabs, probably dating from the twelfth century, commemorate clerics at Selston (Nottinghamshire) and Carisbrooke (Isle of Wight).

Monuments with relief figures appear to have been introduced in the century following the Conquest. Most of the earliest survivals commemorate members of the higher clergy. Near the start of the series are effigies in Westminster Abbey commemorating Abbots Gilbert Crispin (died 1118), Gervase (died 1157) and Laurence (died 1173), as well as those in Salisbury Cathedral (Wiltshire) to Bishops Roger (died 1139) and Jocelyn de Bohun (died 1184), some of which may be retrospective commissions. Following hard on the heels of these is the effigy fragment of *c.* 1180 at Sherborne Abbey (Dorset) commemorating Abbot Clement. Two other figures, both relatively little known, appear to antedate these examples. Sunk within a plain frame and located on the outside east wall of St Nicholas, Bathampton (Somerset), is the figure of an abbot with a crozier supported in the crook of his right arm, holding his right hand in blessing and with a book clasped in his left hand. It may have been removed from nearby Bath Abbey and most likely commemorates Bishop John de Villula (died 1122), whose sepulchre with an effigy was seen in a ruinous condition in the abbey *c.* 1540 by the antiquary John Leland. More unusual is a damaged low-relief effigial slab formerly in Colne Priory (Essex) but now in St Stephen's Chapel, Bures (Suffolk). It commemorates a man in ceremonial or civilian dress, whom the inscription identifies as Aubrey de Vere II, Master

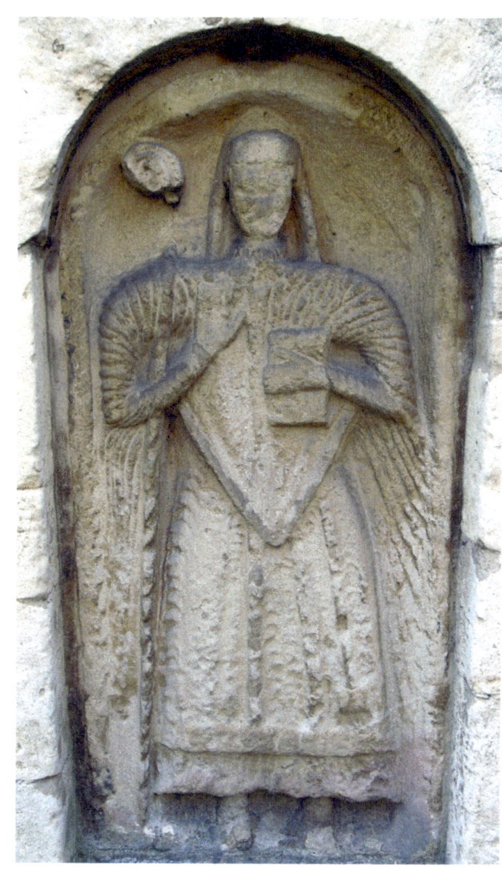

Bathampton (Somerset): possibly originally from Bath Abbey and perhaps commemorating Bishop John de Villula (died 1122).

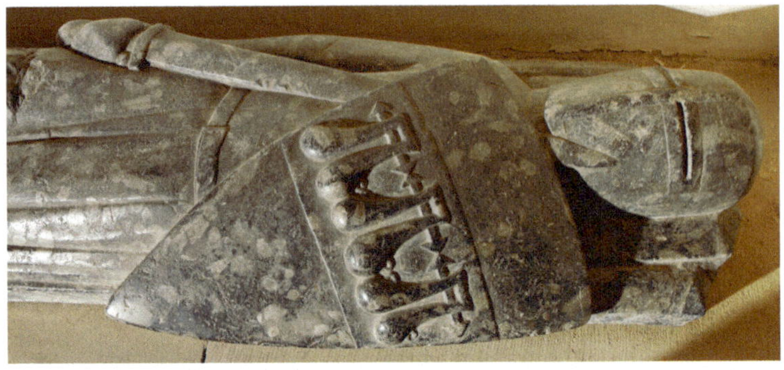

Hurworth-on-Tees (County Durham): Frosterley marble military effigy to a member of the Ros family, wearing a great helm and with his sword upraised.

Chamberlain of England (died 1141), who was founder of the priory. The monument forms part of the pattern of high-status monuments to founders, as exemplified by Gundrada's slab from Lewes Priory. Many other such early effigial monuments may have been destroyed during the dissolution of the monasteries.

Most effigies were carved from limestone or sandstone. Many twelfth- and thirteenth-century examples, however, are in polishable limestones. The attraction of these stones was their dark, reflective surface appearance. The first trendsetter was Tournai marble, a dense blue-black Carboniferous limestone, quarried on the banks of the River Scheldt in Belgium. It was highly regarded and exported to much of northern Europe. Tournai marble was swiftly superseded in England by Purbeck marble, quarried and largely worked near Corfe Castle in the Isle of Purbeck (Dorset), and which gained wide acceptance as a stone suitable for commemorating people of status throughout England. Among the earliest secular effigies carved from Purbeck marble are the much-restored series of military effigies in the Temple church, London. Significant numbers of Purbeck marble effigies to knights, as well as clerics, were commissioned from

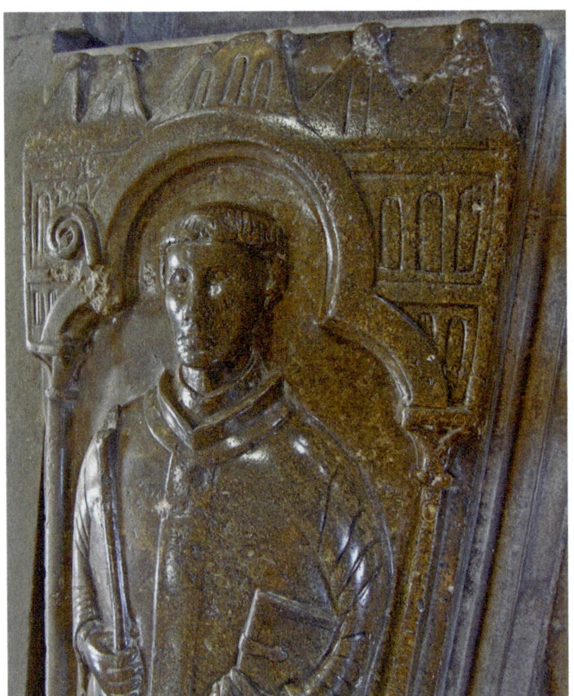

Peterborough Cathedral (Cambridgeshire): Alwalton marble effigy of an unknown abbot.

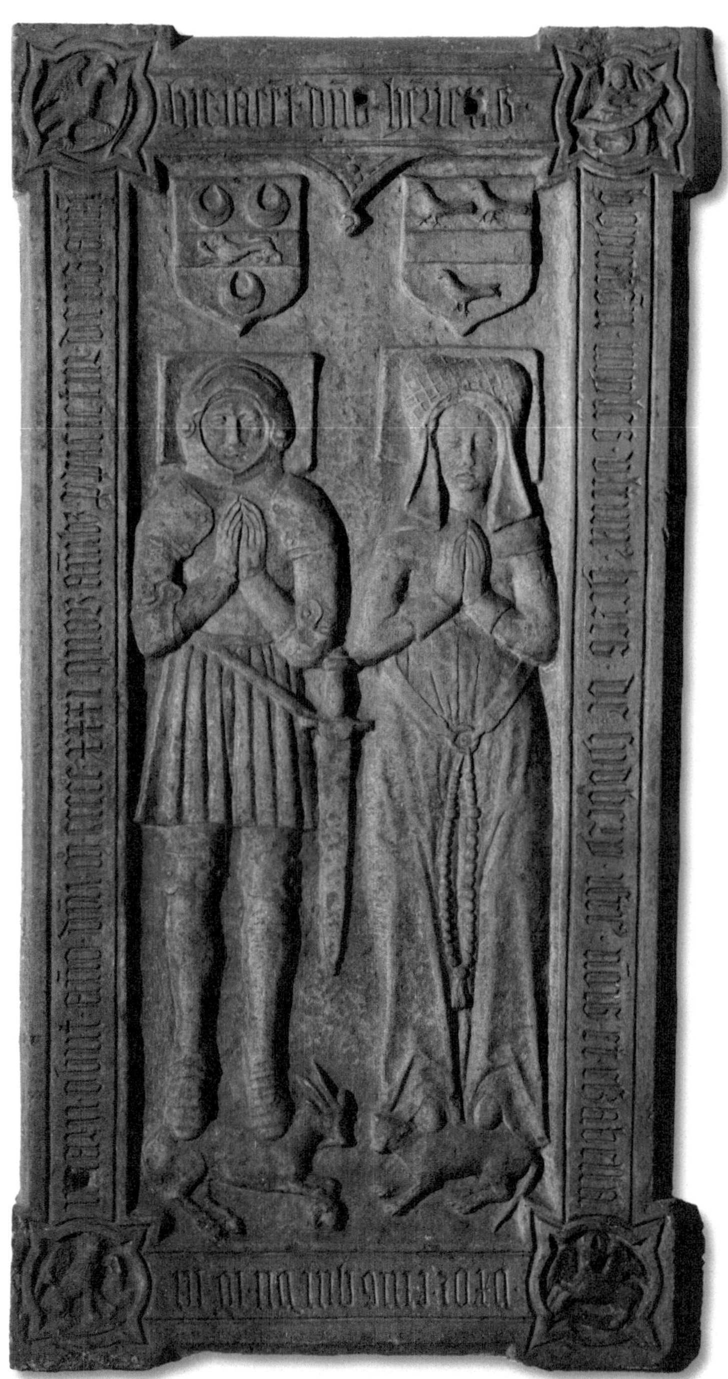

Gilling West (North Yorkshire): low-relief Egglestone marble slab to Sir Henry Boynton and his wife, Isabella (died 1531). They are shown in outmoded costume.

*c.*1230, the stone remaining popular until the 1270s, when the demand for effigies in this material declined. The last surviving mainstream effigies produced in this stone are military monuments of *c.*1325–30 at Conington (Cambridgeshire) and of *c.*1340 at Dodford (Northamptonshire). Other polishable limestones were used as local substitutes for Purbeck marble, including Alwalton marble quarried near Peterborough, Frosterley marble from County Durham, and Egglestone marble quarried on the banks of the River Tees near Barnard Castle (County Durham).

All these polishable limestones were abandoned for producing relief effigies in the early fourteenth century, monuments instead being carved from limestones, sandstones and wood. The shift in usage from sedimentary marbles to these softer materials may well have been prompted by the more widespread use of surface finishes on effigies. If the whole of the stone was to be covered by polychromy (complex painted decoration), there was little point in using the prestigious sedimentary marbles, which would have been more expensive to buy and harder to carve.

At the same time as sedimentary marbles fell from favour, however, a new stone began to be exploited. Alabaster from the Midlands was first used for tombs to royalty and their circle, including Edward II (died 1327)

Guisborough (North Yorkshire): Egglestone marble tomb-chest, known as the Brus cenotaph (c.1520).

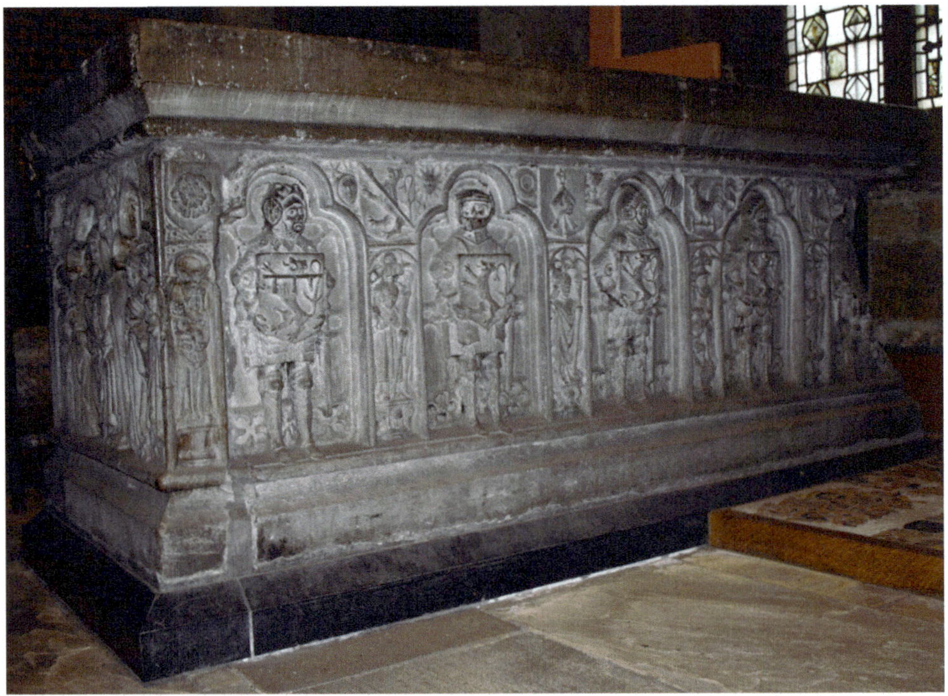

in Gloucester Cathedral, and for the higher clergy, such as Archbishop John Stratford (died 1348) in Canterbury Cathedral (Kent), Bishop William of Edington (died 1366) in Winchester Cathedral (Hampshire) and Archbishop Langham (died 1376) in Westminster Abbey. The use of alabaster for monuments was taken up by the nobility and gentry to become the stone of status up to the Reformation and beyond. It could be carved with exceptionally fine detail; the rendering of armour, costume and jewellery in particular can appear very realistic; hence the carved alabaster tombs of the fifteenth century include some of our most eye-catching effigial monuments.

The late-fourteenth-century satirical poem *Piers the Plowman's Crede* paints a vivid picture of church monuments as they were when first erected. It describes raised tombs, knights in alabaster and marble with coats of arms, and 'lovely ladies ywrought leyen by her sydes, / In many gay garmentes that were gold-beten'. It is clear from this that, for the most part, what we see today is just the bare frame of the monument, with little trace of the brightly coloured and gilded robes described here. Freestone monuments would often have been entirely polychromed to give what medieval people regarded as a realistic impression of a living person. Alabaster monuments would have been more sparingly painted, to allow the translucent beauty of the stone still to be appreciated; alabaster approximates the skin tone, whereas hair, eyes, lips and clothes were more commonly painted, as were costume and details of armour and heraldry.

Some monuments, such as that carved out of oak to Walter de Helyon, a fourteenth-century franklin, at Much Marcle (Herefordshire), have been given a modern coat of paint to give an impression of the original appearance. The colour is in part based on traces of original paint and has some gradation to simulate wear, but the result is lacking in depth and subtlety. Some effigies are known to have been

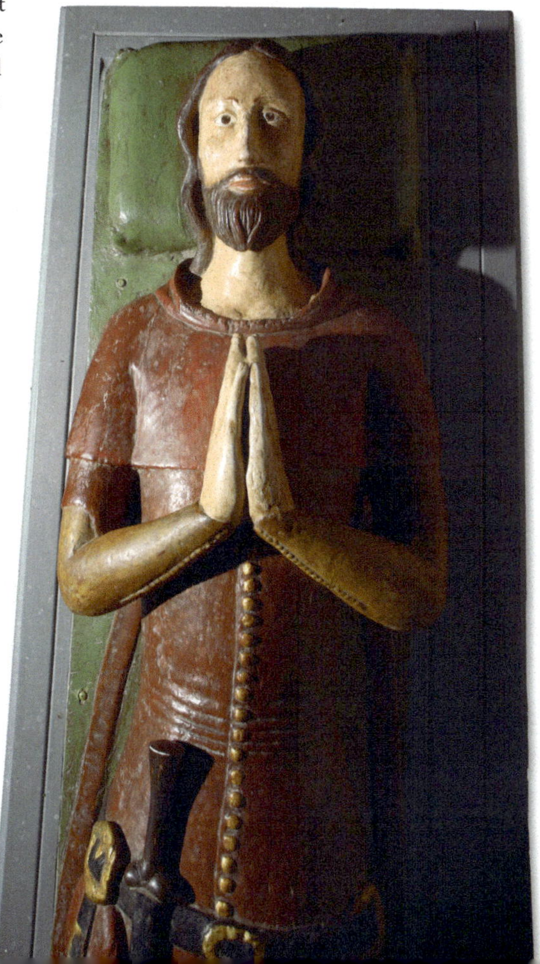

Much Marcle (Herefordshire): wooden effigy to Walter de Helyon (*c.* 1360), a franklin. The paint is modern but based on traces of original polychromy.

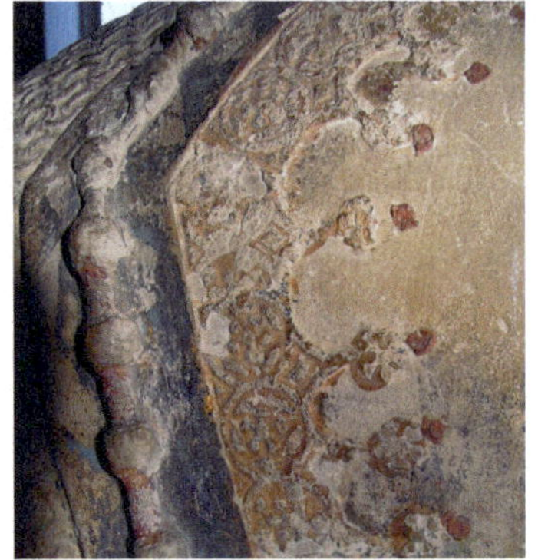

repainted several times, the new colour scheme not always adhering to the previous one. The effigy in Southwark Cathedral (London) to the poet John Gower (died 1408) wears a gown, which was said to be of 'purple damask' in the sixteenth century, scarlet in 1719 and purple in 1765; it is now scarlet with gold motifs.

Medieval polychromy was rich and subtle, requiring the application of multiple coats of tints and glazes that were often superimposed with patterning and – in the case of high-quality effigies – gold and silver leaf. Moulded decoration, tinted wax, fake jewels and enamel plates added to the sumptuous appearance of the finest monuments. Some of the monuments in Westminster Abbey, including those to Edmund Crouchback, Earl of Lancaster (died 1296), and Aymer de Valence, Earl of Pembroke (died 1324), retain much of their original surface finishes, but they are difficult for the general public to see. Good but partial remains can be seen on some tombs in parish churches. Sir Roger de Boys's effigy at Ingham (Norfolk) wears a bacinet with gesso and fictive jewels imitating the borders of high-quality armour, while his wife's headdress is adorned with faux pearls. The effigy of Joan Nevill, wife of William Fitzalan, ninth Earl of Arundel (died 1488), at Arundel (West Sussex) wears an ornate and richly coloured headdress. When first set up, such tombs must have stunned viewers with their magnificence.

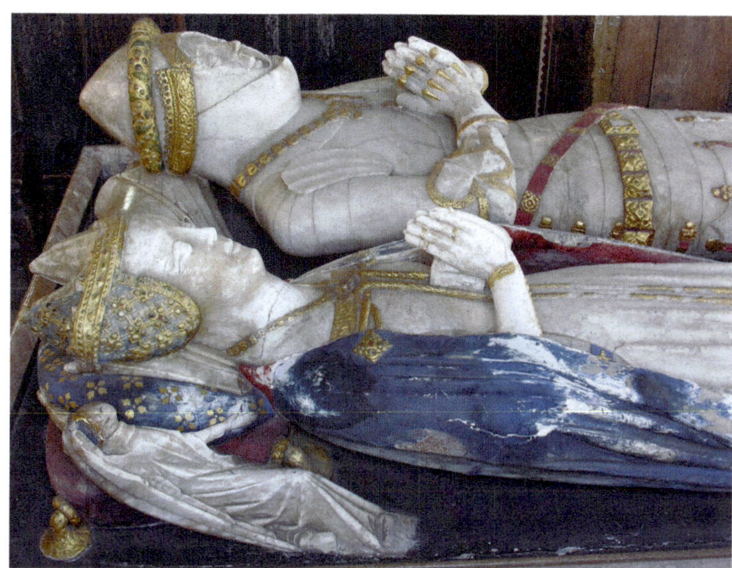

Dennington (Suffolk): William Bardolph (died 1441) was chamberlain to Henry VI, a hero of Agincourt and Harfleur, and a Knight of the Garter.

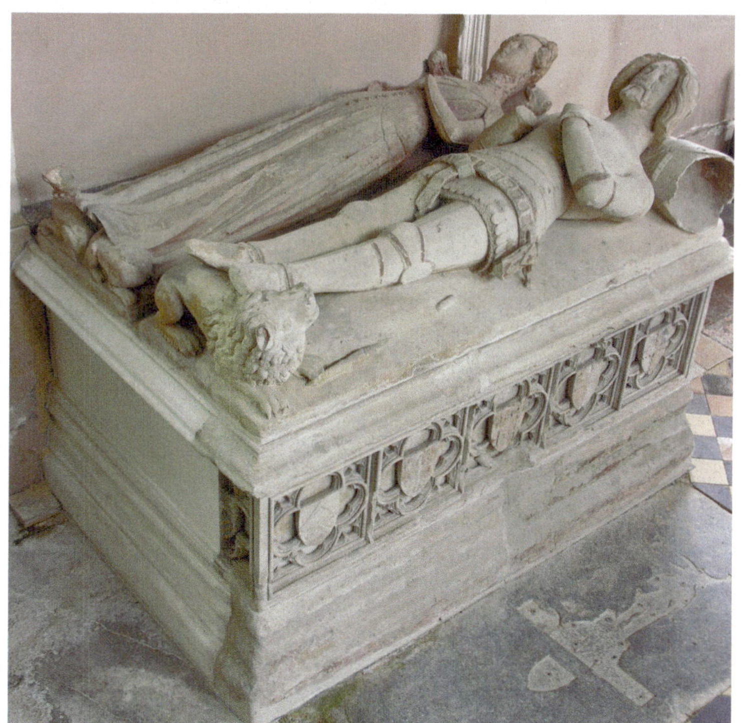

Erwarton (Suffolk): Sir Bartholomew Bacon (died 1392) and his wife, Anne. Close inspection reveals considerable traces of medieval paint.

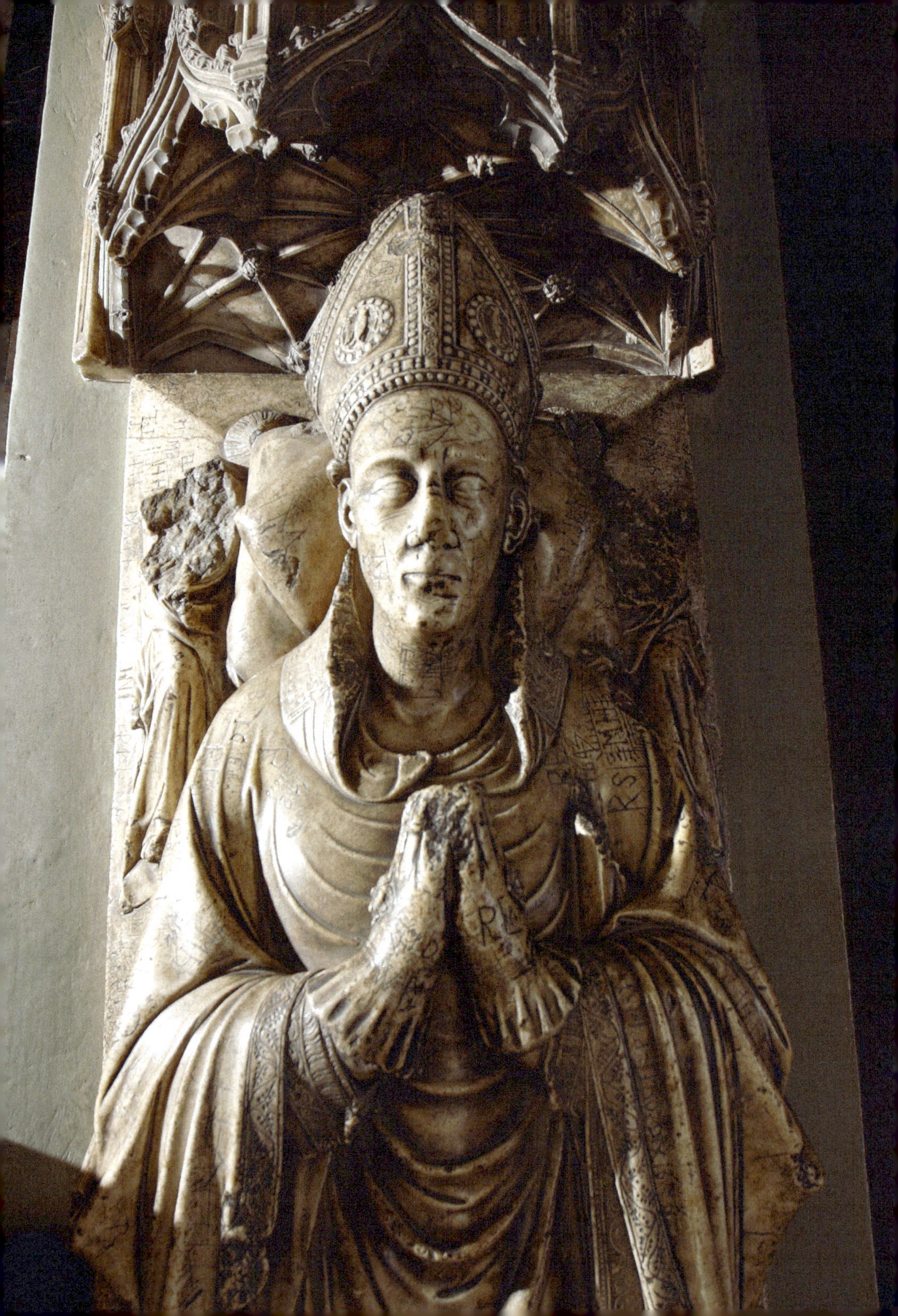

PLACEMENT WITHIN THE CHURCH

Burial and commemoration inside churches were regarded as preferable to churchyard tombs, but the location within the church where a monument was erected was equally significant. The vital consideration was the visibility of the monument to the congregation and, even more importantly, the clergy. If it was prominent, it would be more likely to attract prayers for the soul.

Burial in the chancel was predominantly the prerogative of the clergy, although in parish churches the family which held the manor may also have claimed burial rights there. The position to the north of the altar was a privileged location and thus often reserved for founders. Those who chose burial in the chancel often had to compromise regarding the type of memorial they could choose. In 1474 William Fitzwilliam of Sprotbrough (South Yorkshire) asked to be buried in a manner befitting the lord of the manor in the choir of the church but 'in such a way that those celebrating divine service might not be impeded'. He was commemorated by a floor brass, as were others with the same priorities. The chancel of the collegiate church of Cobham (Kent) is paved by serried ranks of brasses to the Cobham family.

In the late fifteenth century, a highly desirable burial location was on the north side of the altar in a tomb-chest that could also serve as a support for the Easter Sepulchre, in which the crucifix and frequently other sacred elements were deposited from Good Friday to Easter Sunday in commemoration of Christ's entombment and resurrection. The incised slab at Ashby Folville (Leicestershire) to Ralph Wodford (died 1498) is in such a location. It shows him as a cadaver, but he is casting aside his shroud, and the image is accompanied by an inscription asking for prayers for the souls of Ralph and his wife and for their bodily resurrection, together with the familiar text from Job 19: 'I know that my Redeemer liveth…'. The close link between tomb design and location is obvious.

Wealthy men who wanted a high tomb in a position that would attract the attention of the clergy set up chantries in chapels served by dedicated

Allensmore (Herefordshire): Sir Andrew Herley (died 1392) and his wife, Juliana. This is one of a small group of unusual inlaid floor slabs in the county. Note the remains of red colouring in some shields.

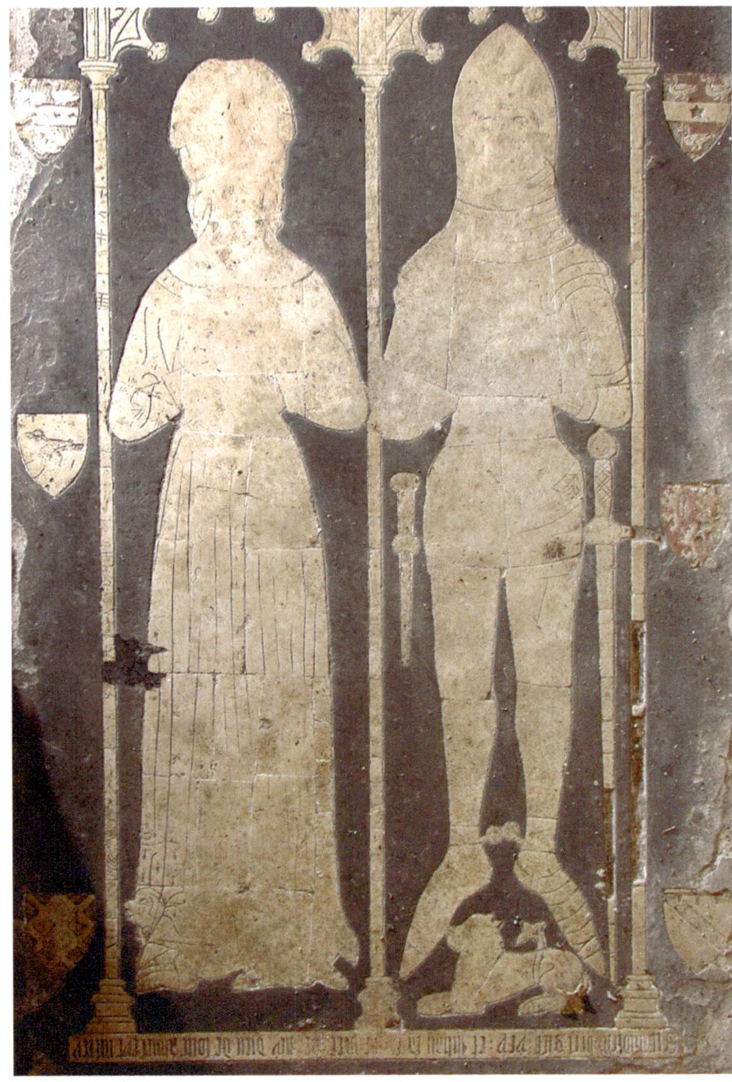

clergy, paid for out of the chantry endowment, who would celebrate daily soul masses. Among the most impressive is the finely furnished Beauchamp chantry chapel at Warwick, purpose-built and set apart from the rest of the church. Many of England's cathedrals, notably Winchester, have a series of stone-cage chantries running down the aisles, each one a miniature powerhouse of prayer. They are notable for their impressive architecture but inside they are claustrophobic, having room for little more than the tomb, the altar and piscina, and the celebrant. At a parish level some chantries were established by partitioning off part of the existing fabric to make a private chapel. The parclose screens were commonly constructed from wood, as still seen at Dennington (Suffolk), but most were destroyed, along with the fittings, at the dissolution of the chantries in Edward VI's reign; hence we have little visible sign that they were ever there. Some contain just the effigies of the founders, as with that at Pucklechurch (Gloucestershire) to William de Cheltenham (died *c.*1371–4), steward to the powerful Berkeley family, and his wife. Others developed into family mausolea, including the Cockayne chapel at Ashbourne (Derbyshire), and the Herbert Chapel at

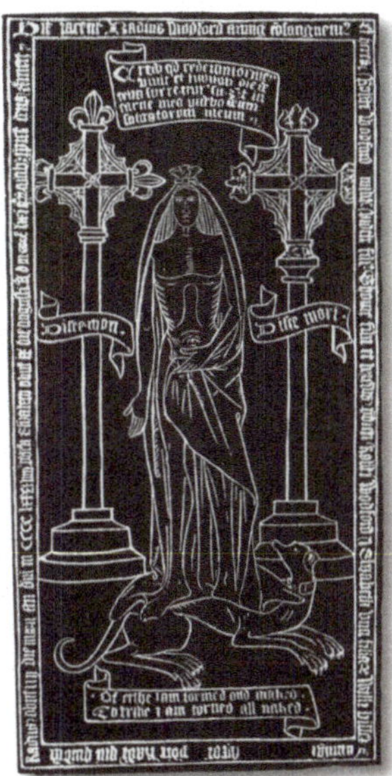

Ashby Folville (Leicestershire): Ralph Wodford (died 1498). His incised slab combines a cadaver effigy with Resurrection imagery.

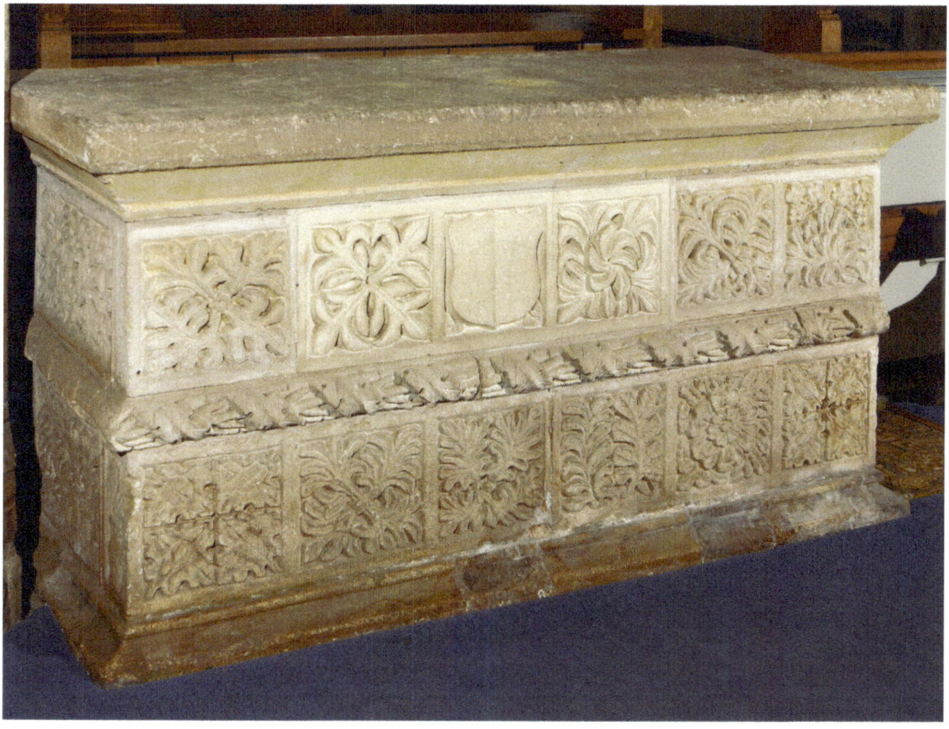

Luccombe (Somerset): tomb-chest of the first half of the sixteenth century. The carving is vernacular in style but vigorously executed. It was originally in the position associated with Easter sepulchres.

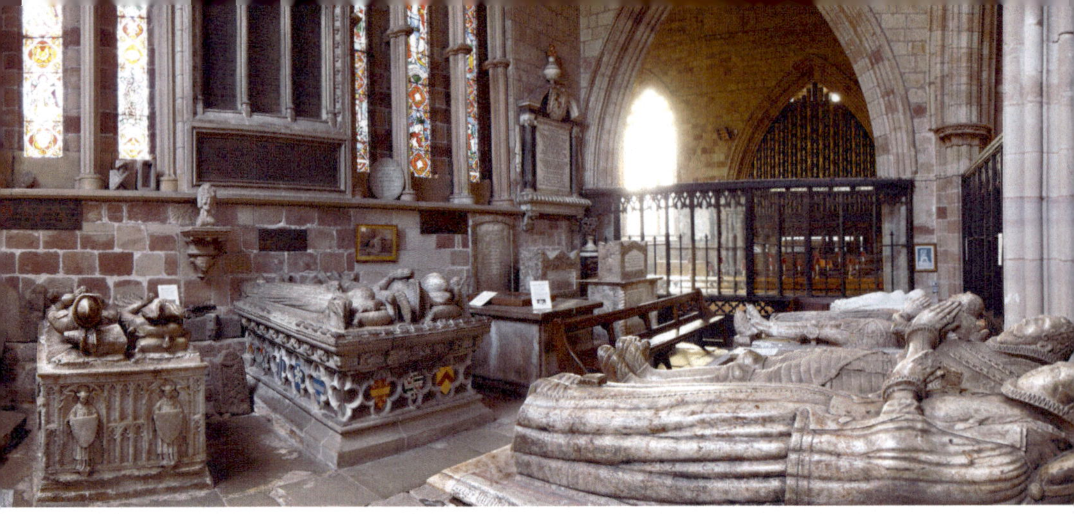

Abergavenny (Monmouthshire), both of which are crowded with monuments.

Evidence from wills reveals the preferred burial locations of those who could not provide their own chapel. Many asked for burial and commemoration near the graves of family members. Nicholas Blackburn junior (died 1448), merchant of York, touchingly chose burial 'in the choir of St Mary where I was accustomed to sit within my parish church of All Saints in North Street in York near the tomb of my children buried there'. Locations near altars and devotional images of saints were considered desirable. In 1486 William Stokker, knight and alderman of London, requested burial in St Michael's church 'before the image of seint George', and that he should have made thereby 'a litell tombe in the wall'. Again, the 1507 will of Richard Genne, vicar of Willesborough (Kent), requests burial 'in the choir ... before the statue of the Blessed Virgin Mary ... for my

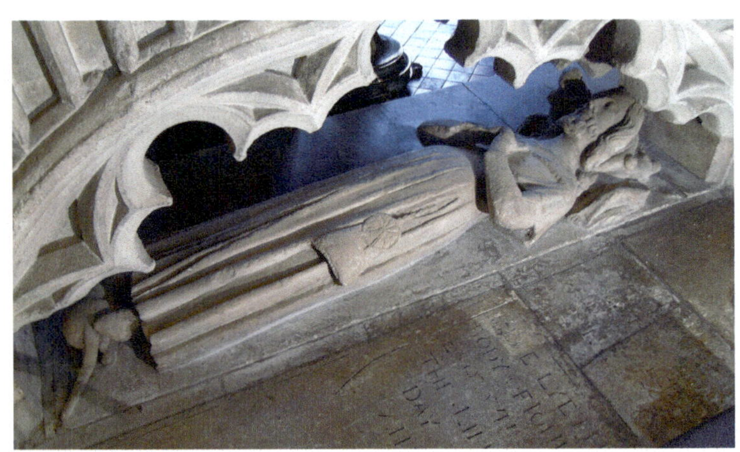

sepulchre called my epitaph an image of the Blessed Mary and figure of my body kneeling before the image'. As with Ralph Wodford's incised slab, the design of Genne's monument was chosen to reflect its intended location. None of these three monuments survives, but these and other wills remind us when we look at tombs that their locations were subject to careful thought.

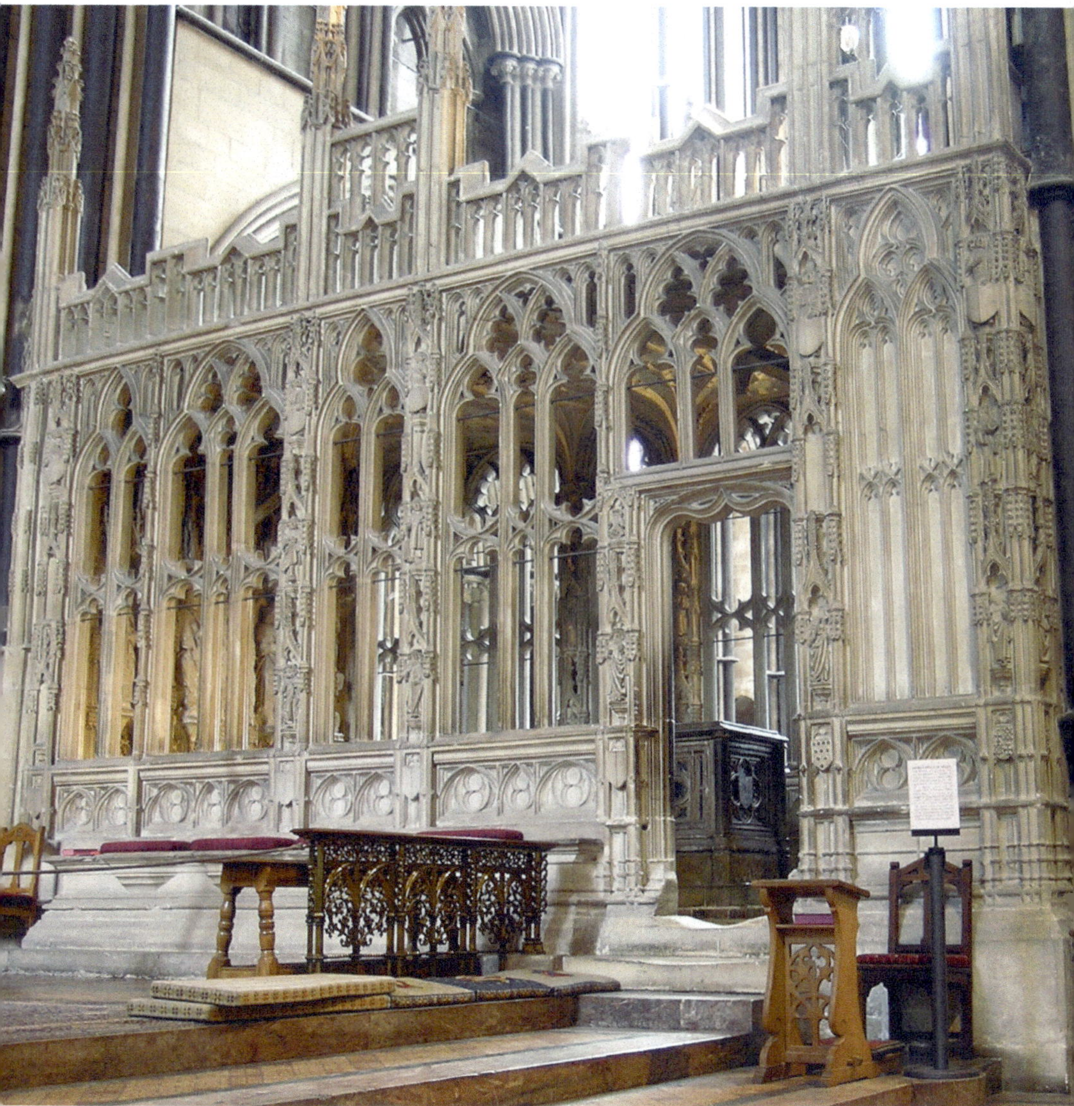

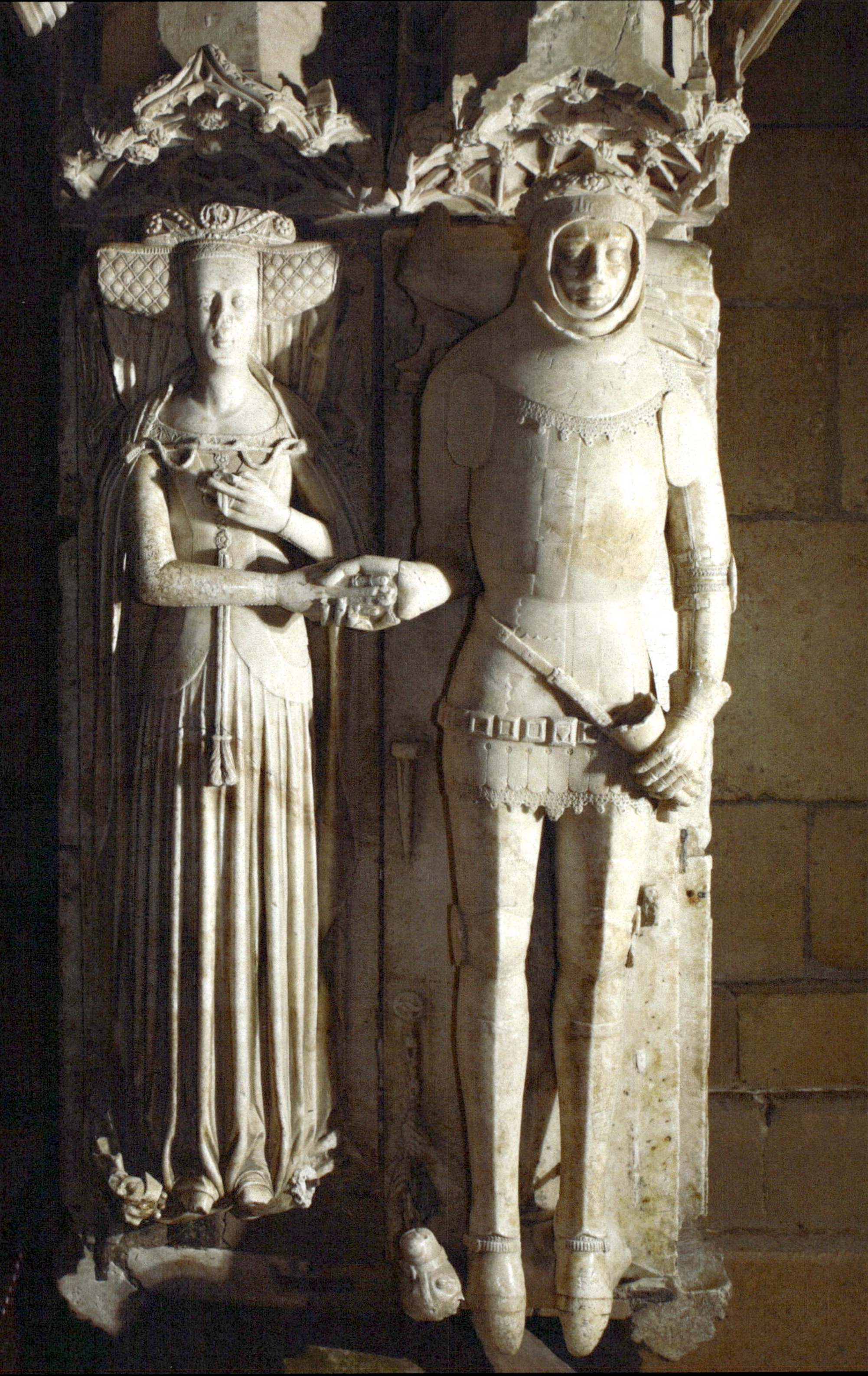

CHOICES IN TOMB DESIGN

THE MOST evocative monuments are of men shown in armour. They are commonly referred to as knights and thought of as fighting men, but not all the men commemorated by such monuments were strictly of knightly status, and neither were they all soldiers. Such tombs can commemorate men of higher social status, such as barons, earls and dukes, or of lower social status. In the contract for the making of the alabaster tomb of Ralph Greene esquire (died 1417) and his widow, Katherine, at Lowick (Northamptonshire), she specified that her late husband should be shown as 'the counterfeit of an esquire, armed at all points'. The makers, Thomas Prentys and Robert Sutton, alabasterers of Chellaston (Derbyshire), who were responsible for a series of fine alabaster tombs, provided a figure indistinguishable from those produced for clients of higher status. The commemorated are always shown on their tombs in attire appropriate to their status in life, and being armour-clad identified them as forming part of the dominant landed and politically active second estate in society.

Military monuments may display other distinct characteristics. Although many knights are shown with their hands in prayer, this became standard only after the mid-fourteenth century. Before then, many are shown in the act of drawing or sheathing their sword; their crossed legs – not an indicator of participation in crusades as once believed – add further to the impression of the ever-vigilant warrior, ready to spring into action. Among the most contorted and seemingly restless of such figures are the fine tombs in wood to Robert Curthose, Duke of Normandy (died 1134), at Gloucester Cathedral, and in stone to William de Valence the Younger (died 1282) in Dorchester Abbey (Oxfordshire). Different in conception, but perhaps with the same intention, the effigy at Ottery St Mary (Devon) of Sir Otho de Grandison (died 1358), a veteran of Crécy, has his sword tucked at the ready under his left arm.

Among the accoutrements of the warrior knight was the warhorse. So important was this to the chivalric ideal that during aristocratic funerals horses were often brought into church bearing the arms and armour of the deceased.

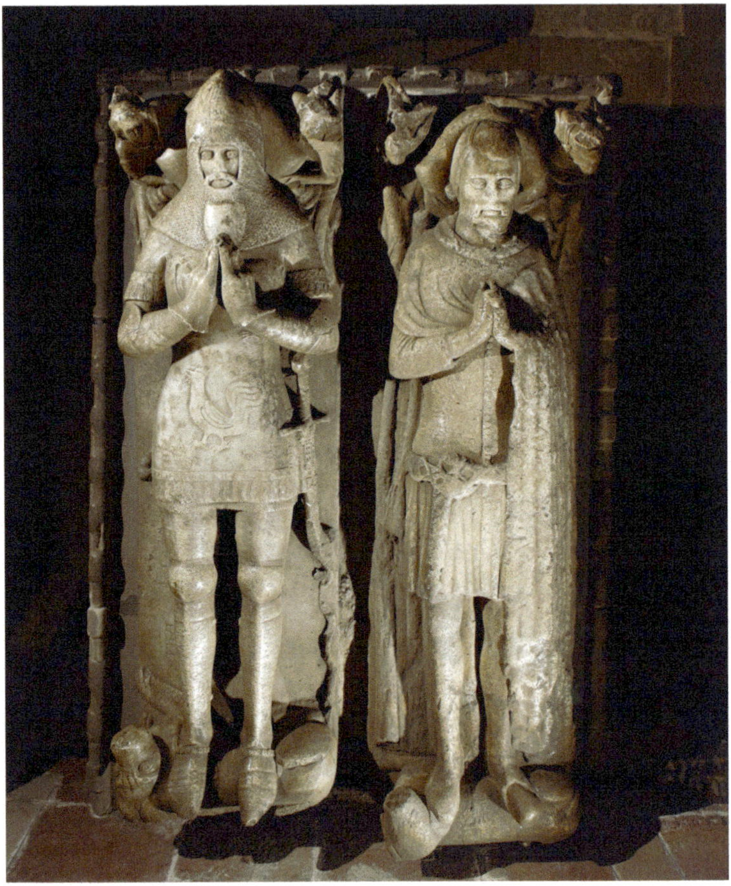

Right: Ashbourne (Derbyshire): John Cockayne I was shown with a coif indicating his profession as a lawyer, while his son, Edmund (died 1403), who married an heiress, is in armour.

Below: Dorchester Abbey (Oxfordshire): William de Valence the Younger (died 1282). He is shown in an extremely contorted pose.

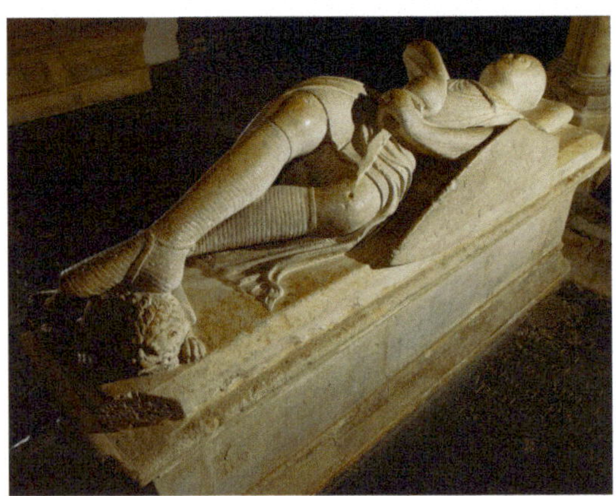

Warhorses feature on a few English tombs, although they are more common in Italy. The earliest is a mid-thirteenth-century Purbeck marble coffin lid at Hampstead Norreys (Berkshire) which features, above a huge shield, a low-relief carving of a knight on horseback, with his lance ready to meet the enemy. Horses accompanied by esquires form the footrests for the effigies of Sir Robert Stapledon (died 1320) in Exeter Cathedral (Devon) and of a member of the Sleyt family at Old Somerby

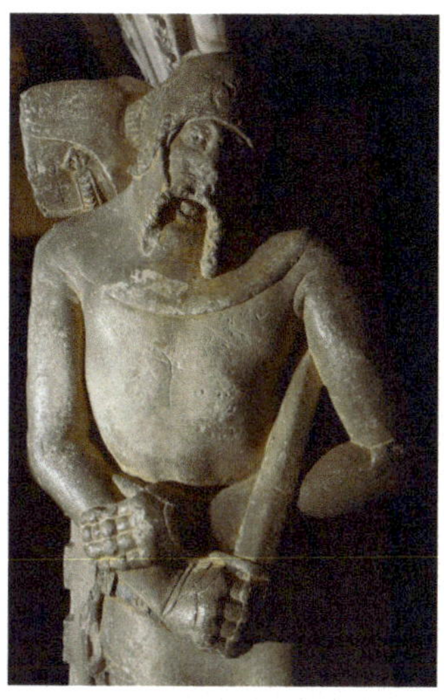

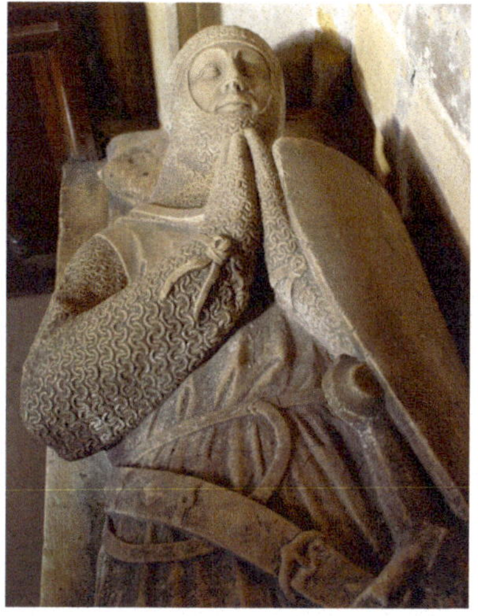

Far left: Ottery St Mary (Devon): Sir Otho de Grandison (died 1358) – among the best south-western tombs of this date. Otho is shown with his sword tucked under his arm.

Left: Felixkirk (North Yorkshire): unknown knight. One of the best-preserved fourteenth-century military effigies in England.

(Lincolnshire). The head of a horse features on a semi-effigial slab at Gilling East (North Yorkshire), along with a shield with the arms of Belkamore and a sword, and on the effigy at Minster-in-Sheppey (Kent) to Sir Robert de Shurland (died 1333), a veteran of the Scottish wars of Edward I and II, who is shown lying on his shield and carrying a lance. Other echoes of the chivalric ideal are found on effigies at Bawdrip (Somerset) and Puddletown (Dorset), on which instead of a conventional shield there is shown one with a 'bouche', an inlet designed to receive a couched lance before impact.

Some men chose to immortalise their military careers and their companions-in-arms by the use of heraldry on tomb-chests. An outstanding example is the tomb at Lingfield (Surrey) to Reginald, Lord Cobham (died 1361), one of Edward III's leading companions and campaigners. The monument at Bunbury (Cheshire) to Sir Hugh Calverley (died 1394), a mercenary, alternates his arms with those of his brother-in-arms Sir Robert Knolles (died 1407). Another interesting feature was for some military effigies of the first half of the fifteenth century to have an abbreviated form of the words 'Jesus of Nazareth' carved on the

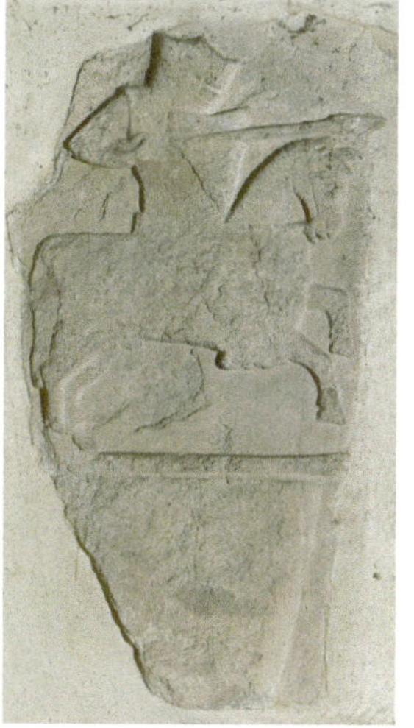

Hampstead Norreys (Berkshire): mid-thirteenth-century Purbeck marble coffin lid, which features, above a huge shield, a low-relief carving of a knight on horseback.

Right: Exeter Cathedral (Devon): Sir Robert Stapledon (died 1320). At his feet is an esquire holding the reins of his master's warhorse.

Far right: Minster-in-Sheppey (Kent): Sir Robert de Shurland (died 1333). He lies on his shield and holds a lance.

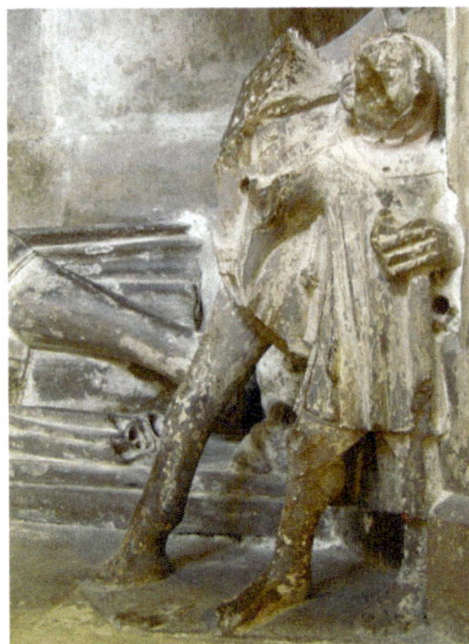

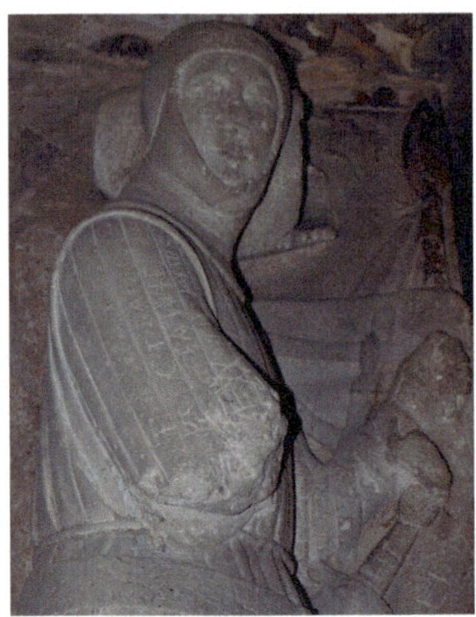

bacinet. It was believed that this afforded protection from sudden death. More curious is the mid-fourteenth-century knight at Wilsthorpe (Lincolnshire), a member of the Mortimer family; the hem of his coat armour bears the pithy utterance 'Better is pys [peace] than wers [wars]', possibly the motto of a tournament team.

Bottesford (Leicestershire): William, Lord Roos (died 1414). He has an abbreviated form of the words 'Jesus of Nazareth' carved on the bacinet.

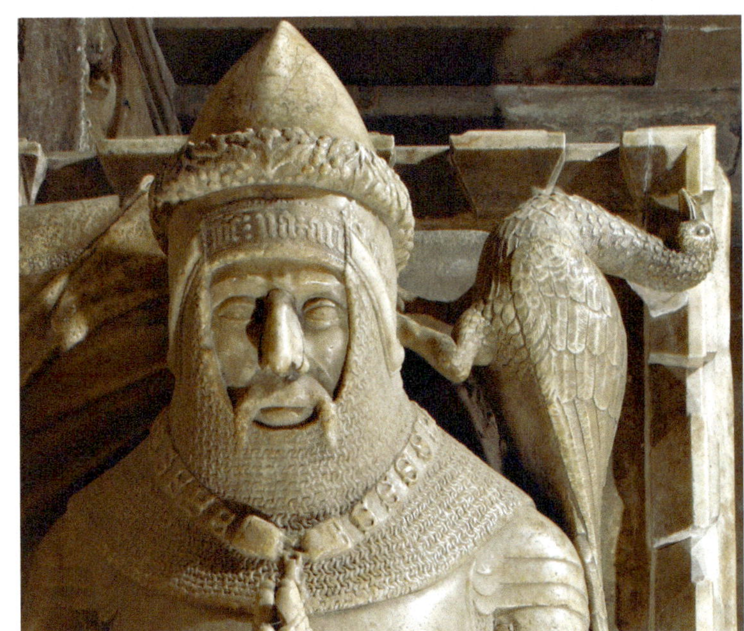

The higher clergy were often trendsetters in tomb design, but their monuments display contradictions in their value systems. Some orders, such as the Cistercians, frowned on sumptuous tombs; many therefore chose simple crozier slabs, as at Egglestone Abbey (County Durham) and Sulby Abbey (Northamptonshire), but by the late fifteenth century their tombs could be as elaborate as those of other orders. Humility may have prompted the simple brass effigial representation at Salisbury Cathedral (Wiltshire) of bishops Ghent (died 1315) and Martival (died 1330), although these brasses were set within an elaborate architectural framework. Others of the higher clergy vied to outdo each other with the splendour of their tombs, with massive canopies reaching almost to the ceiling of the building in which they are housed. The tombs of many Archbishops of Canterbury are a prime example of this. An interesting insight is provided by Robert Winchelsea's letter of 1302 condemning the monument prepared for Bishop Gifford of Worcester because it overshadowed the nearby shrine of St Oswald, kept daylight from the high altar and took the place previously occupied by a bishop popularly regarded as a saint. Winchelsea's own tomb at Canterbury was destroyed in the sixteenth century but is recorded as being 'a right godly tumbe of marble' under a high gabled wall recess.

Initially laymen and their wives were commemorated by separate monuments. Double monuments are believed to have first appeared in the late thirteenth century. Among the most interesting are those which show the couple holding hands. The earliest example, probably from the early fourteenth century, is at Winterbourne Bassett (Wiltshire), but the pose was not taken up again until the 1360s. Its significance is uncertain since we know so little of the private lives of those commemorated, although some examples certainly signify marital love. The contracts for the magnificent copper-alloy tomb costing £950 in Westminster Abbey commissioned by Richard II on the death in 1394 of his beloved queen, Anne of Bohemia, stipulate that the effigies should be hand-clasped. Virtually all examples are

Wilsthorpe (Lincolnshire): mid-fourteenth-century effigy to a member of the Mortimer family. The heraldry is recut, but the text 'Better is pys [peace] than wers [wars]' is original.

Welwick (Yorkshire East Riding): portion of an early-fourteenth-century incised crozier slab.

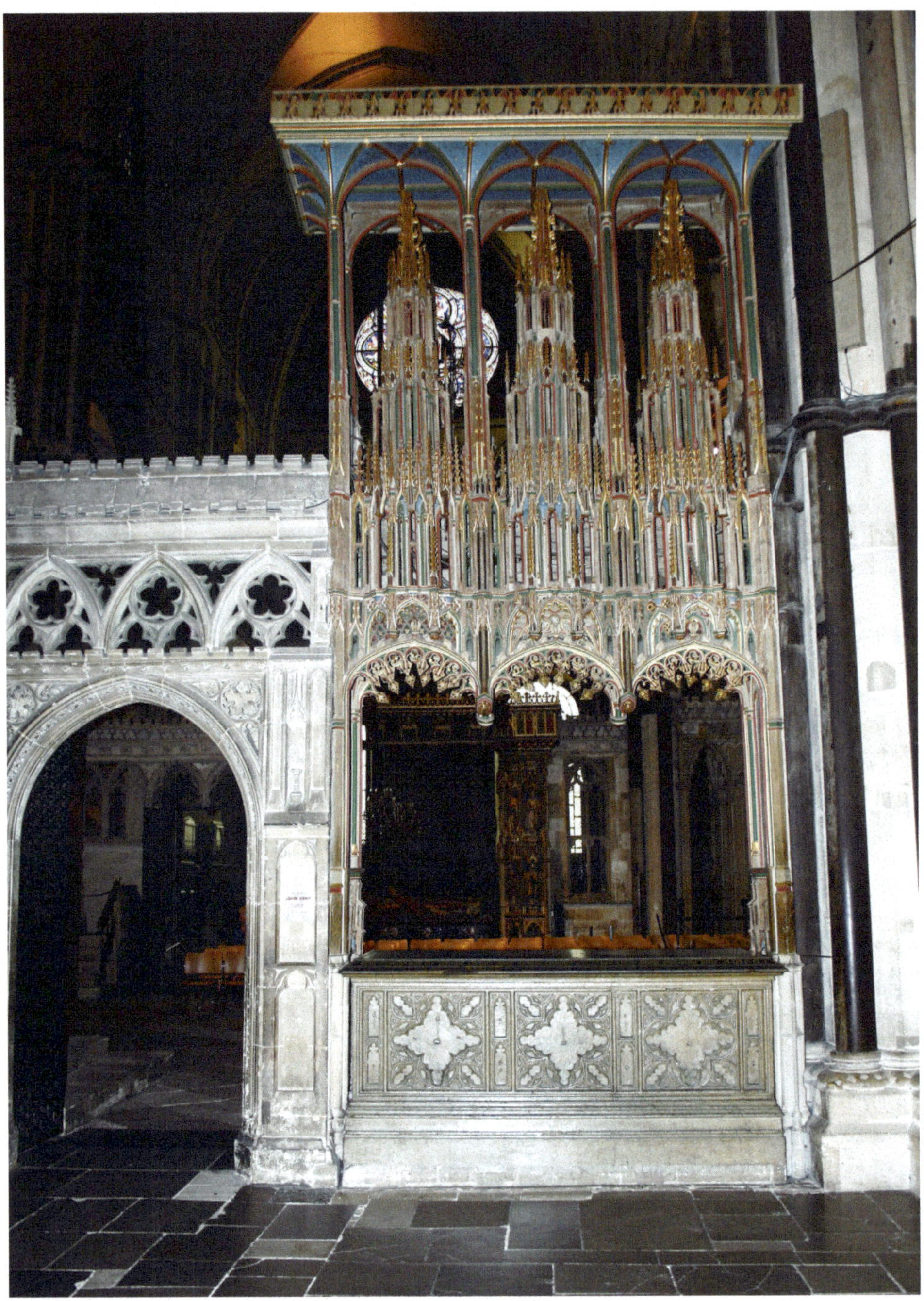

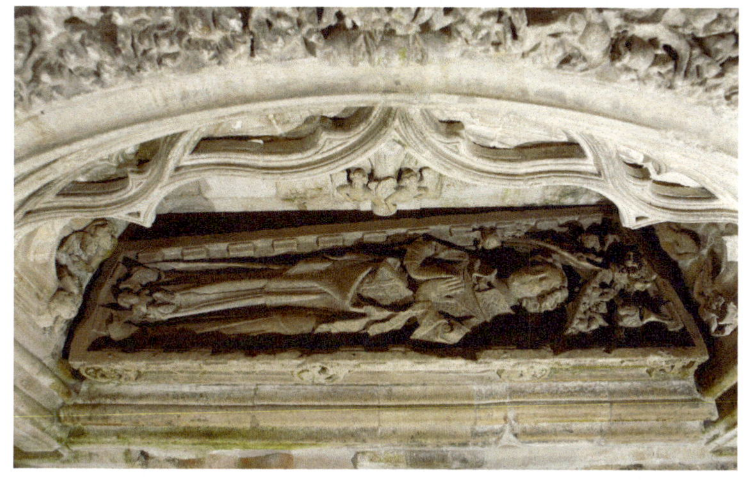

Left: Welwick (Yorkshire East Riding): a priest, perhaps William de la Mare (died 1358). The tomb features an elaborate low-relief effigy.

Opposite: Canterbury Cathedral (Kent): Archbishop John Kemp (died 1454). The high canopy of this splendid tomb reaching almost to the ceiling is typical of archiepiscopal tombs at Canterbury.

of relatively high-status couples with the man shown in armour, a rare exception being the brass at Owston (South Yorkshire) to the Lancastrian esquire Robert Haitfield, which was engraved on the death in 1409 of his wife, Ada; in the inscription the pair are described as 'fully in right love'.

From the early fifteenth century brasses and incised slabs often showed groups of children as miniature figures below their parents, but this imagery was hard to translate to carved tombs, except for representation on the tomb-chest, as exemplified by the tomb of Edward III at Westminster Abbey. A novel solution was adopted at Lowthorpe (Yorkshire East Riding); Sir Thomas de Heslerton (died *c.* 1350) and his wife are shown recumbent

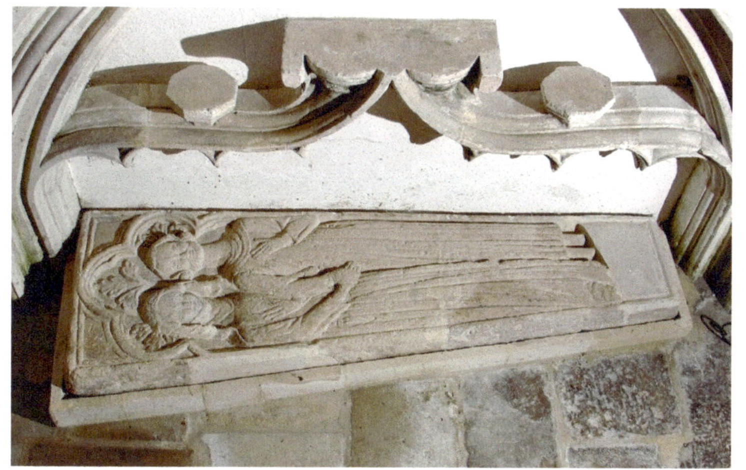

Winterbourne Bassett (Wiltshire): an unknown civilian and his wife, dating from the early fourteenth century. The earliest known example of the hand-holding pose.

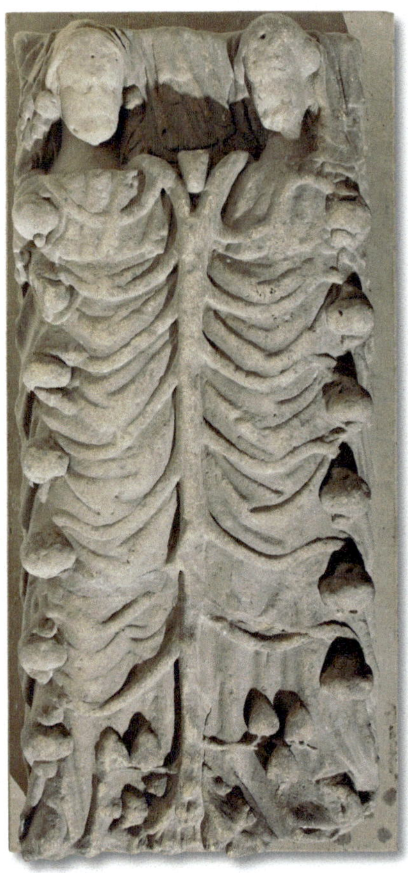

Lowthorpe (Yorkshire East Riding): Sir Thomas de Heslerton (died c.1350) and his wife, shown under a blanket with a tree of Jesse representation of their children over them.

under a blanket on top of which is a tree of Jesse, its branches ending in human heads representing their thirteen children. There are some particularly affecting monuments showing mothers with children. The composition of a monument, probably of late-thirteenth-century date, at Scarcliffe (Derbyshire) to a woman named Constancia and her son John may be based on images of the Blessed Virgin Mary holding the Christ Child. At Bodenham (Herefordshire) a boy peeps out from his mother's mantle (cloak), and a semi-effigy at Howell (Lincolnshire) has one aperture for the mother and another for her child.

Among the most puzzling and misunderstood of monuments are miniature effigies, which are commonly described as being monuments to children. Some undoubtedly commemorate those who died young, such as the alabaster effigy in York Minster to Prince William of Hatfield (died 1337), although he is shown as an adolescent despite being just a few months old when he died. Miniature effigies showing children dressed as young adults, such as those in Westminster Abbey to Edward III's children Blanche of the Tower and William of Windsor, both of whom failed to reach maturity, have led to the mistaken assumption that all undersized effigies commemorate children. Some such tombs have attracted imaginative legends to explain their appearance, including the so-called 'Boy Bishop' in Salisbury Cathedral (Wiltshire). The over-imaginative recutting of a miniature effigy at Elford (Staffordshire) so that he appears to hold a ball was based on an absurd but persistent legend that he was killed by a ball. In fact, many such small effigies mark heart or entrail burials; burial of these organs separate from the remainder of the body enabled multiple commemorations at different locations, increasing the opportunities of prayers for the soul, a practice which was discouraged by a papal bull of 1299. Hence, the inscription on the miniature effigy of a bishop at Abbey Dore (Herefordshire) records that it covers the heart of Bishop John de Breton (died 1275). Some effigies marking heart burials show the deceased holding a heart, while a lady at Coberley (Gloucestershire) inserts her hand into her bodice as if to indicate her heart. Not all effigies holding hearts cover heart burials, however, as it also symbolised Christian faith.

Even more bizarre to modern eyes is the taste for monuments that show the deceased as an emaciated corpse or skeleton. Some 175 such monuments are known of in England, ranging from shroud brasses and incised slabs to elaborate 'double-decker' tombs. Many commemorate those close to the Lancastrian court, including members of the higher clergy. One of the earliest of the 'double-decker' type in England, commemorating Archbishop Chichele (died 1443) in Canterbury Cathedral (Kent), was constructed in his own lifetime. A variety of explanations of their meaning has been postulated, but the most likely is that they acted as a *memento mori*: in the words on the cadaver

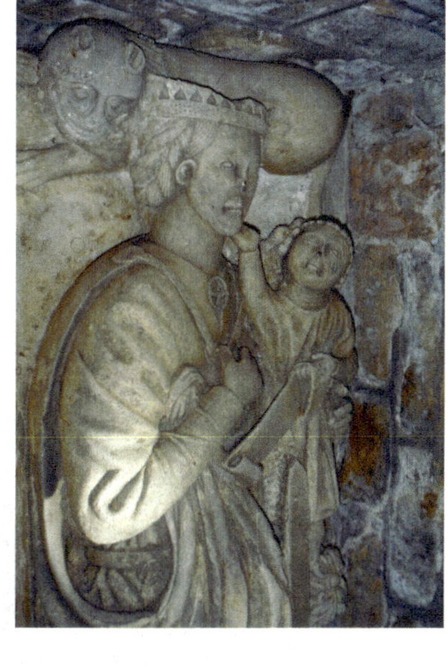

Scarcliffe (Derbyshire): a woman named Constancia and her son, John. This posture may be based on images of the Blessed Virgin Mary holding the Christ Child.

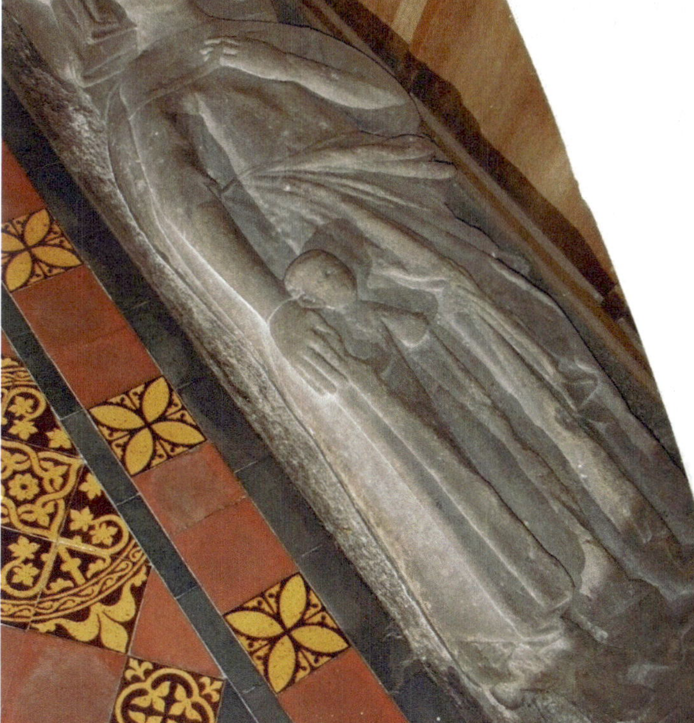

Bodenham (Herefordshire): a boy peeps out from under his mother's mantle.

Right: Haccombe (Devon): an undersized alabaster effigy of *c.* 1370, probably to a child.

Opposite top left: Salisbury Cathedral (Wiltshire): the so-called 'Boy Bishop'. This miniature effigy probably covers the bones of Bishop William de la Corner, who died abroad in 1291.

Opposite top centre: Coberley (Gloucestershire): miniature effigy marking the heart burial of an unknown woman.

Opposite top far right: Sheriff Hutton (North Yorkshire): this undersized alabaster effigy was traditionally thought to commemorate Richard III's son, Edward of Middleham (died 1484), but actually dates from around 1415.

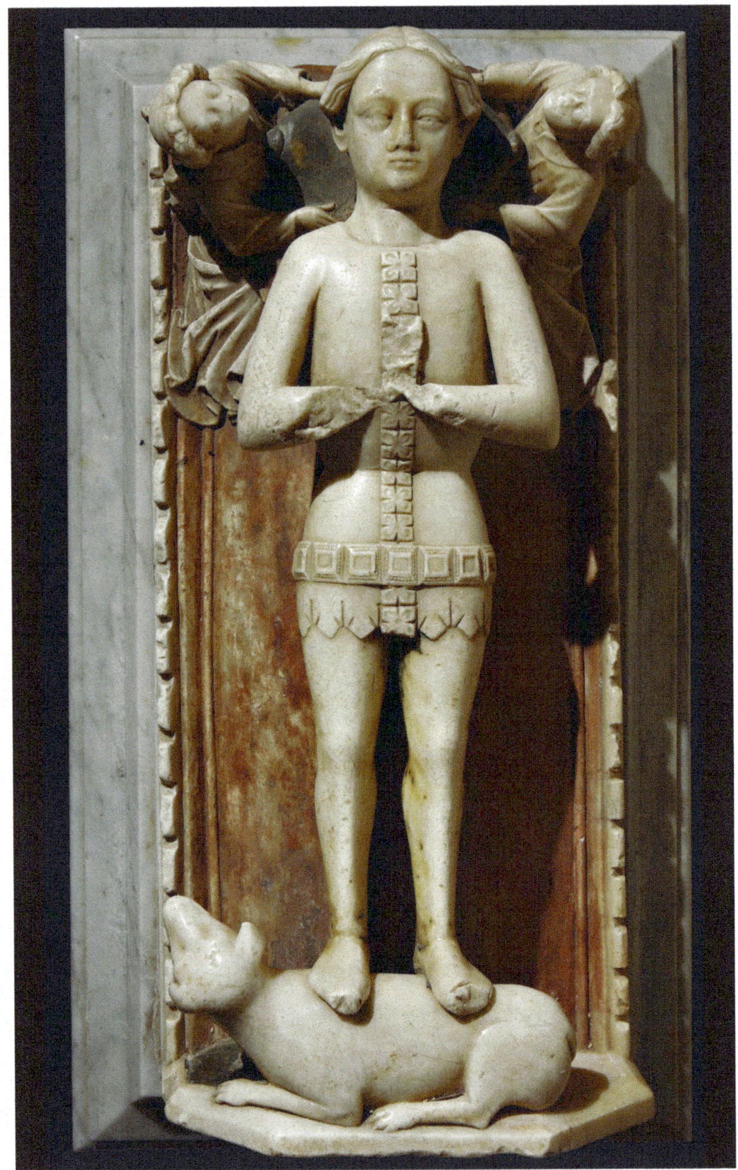

monument in Exeter Cathedral (Devon) to Precentor William Sylke (died 1508), 'I am what you will be and I once was what you are now'. The inscription on the cadaver monument in Bury St Edmunds (Suffolk) to John Baret (died 1467) reflects the sentiments of the fifteenth-century lyric

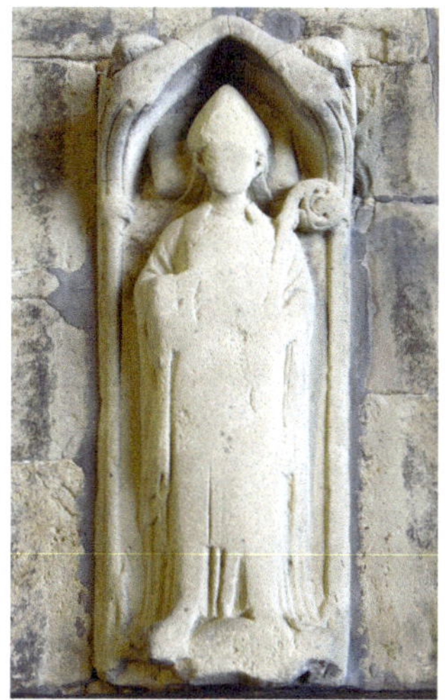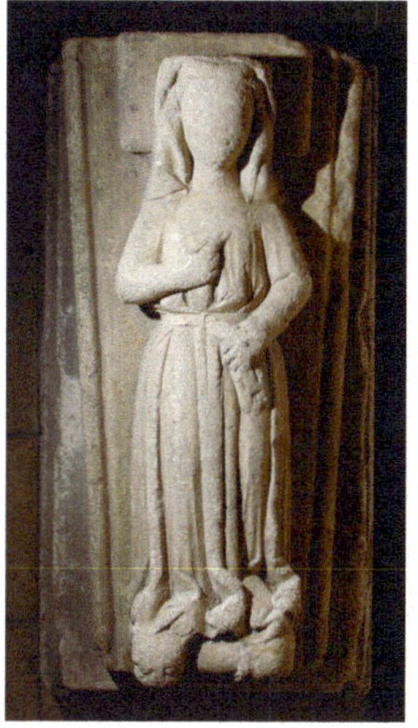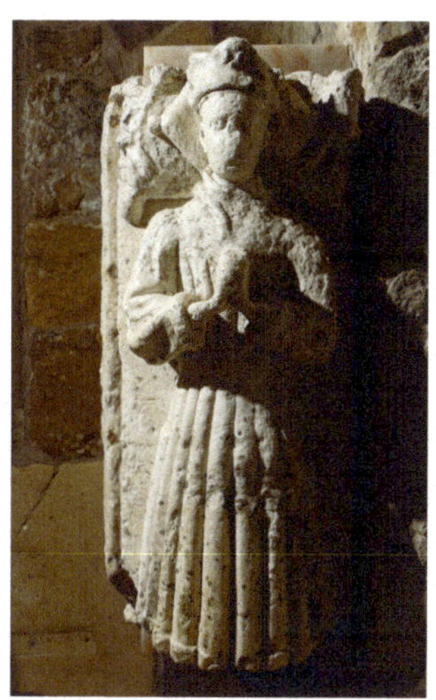

poem *The Mirror of Mortality*: 'He that wil sadly beholde one with his ie [eye] / May se hys own merowr [mirror] and learn for to die'. Yet these were not messages of hopelessness, but a lesson for the onlooker, encouraging him to mend any sinful ways and also prompting him to pray for the deceased. Many cadaver monuments have associated salvific imagery, carrying the message that Christ's redeeming power will lead to our resurrection.

Below:
Bury St Edmunds (Suffolk): cadaver monument to John Baret (died 1467).

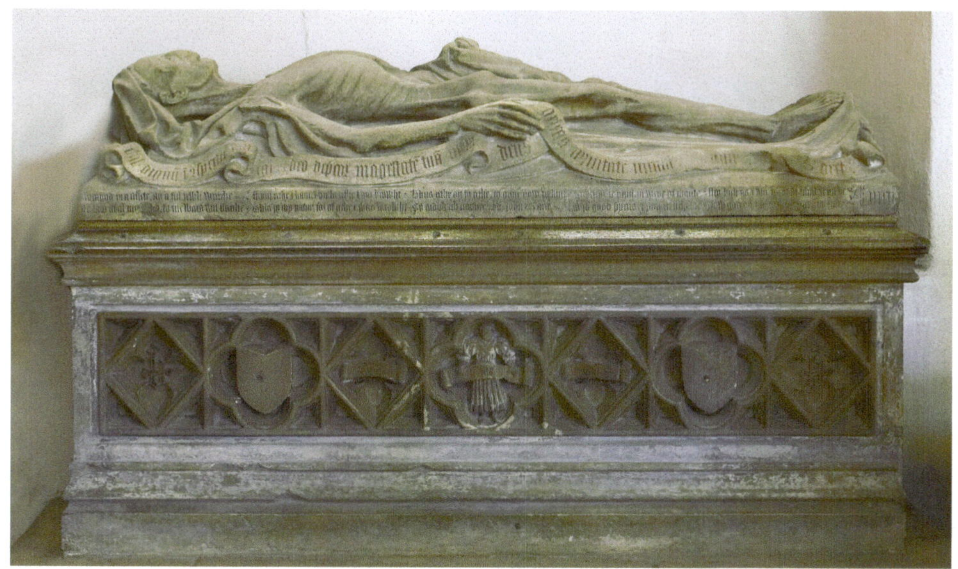

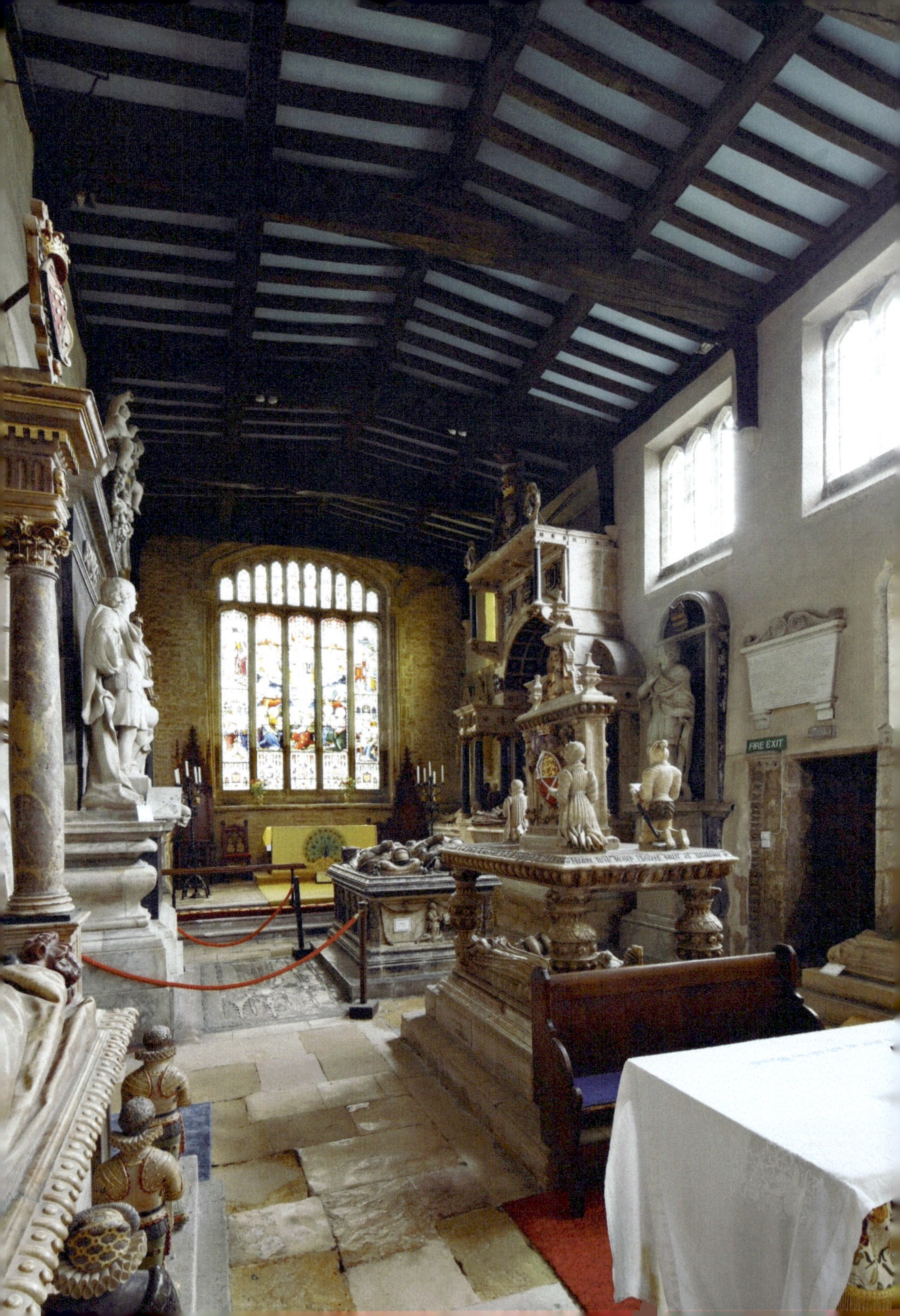

TOMB DESTRUCTION AND MUTILATION

IN HIS narrative poem *Rokeby*, Sir Walter Scott described the tomb destruction that took place at Egglestone Abbey (County Durham) following the dissolution of the monasteries:

> The Civil fury of the time
> Made sport of sacrilegious crime;
> For dark Fanaticism rent
> Altar, and screen, and ornament,
> And peasant hands the tombs o'erthrew
> Of Bowes, of Rokeby, and Fitz-Hugh.

The abbey ruins now contain just a few medieval floor slabs and a tomb-chest commemorating Sir Ralph Bowes (died 1482), but even a minor religious house such as this would once have had many more monuments. In the London Greyfriars' church all the tombs were pulled down and sold for £50. This wholesale destruction was repeated throughout the country, undoubtedly with massive losses of monuments. Even some tombs to royalty failed to escape destruction; Reformation losses include those of Richard III at Leicester, Henry I at Reading (Berkshire), Stephen and his queen, Matilda, at Faversham (Kent) and the retrospective monument to Arthur at Glastonbury (Somerset). This wholesale destruction also resulted in the loss of a disproportionately large number of tombs to the nobility, whose wills show that they were much more likely to opt for burial in religious houses and only in the fifteenth century turned instead in significant numbers to commemoration in parish churches. The abundance of rich monuments in monastic churches that were retained, such as Westminster Abbey and Tewkesbury Abbey, bears this out.

Some tombs were rescued from the remaining monastic and friary churches and moved to parish churches. Thomas Manners, first Earl of Rutland, caused monuments of his ancestors in Belvoir Priory and Croxton Abbey to be moved to the remodelled chancel at Bottesford (Leicestershire), where they

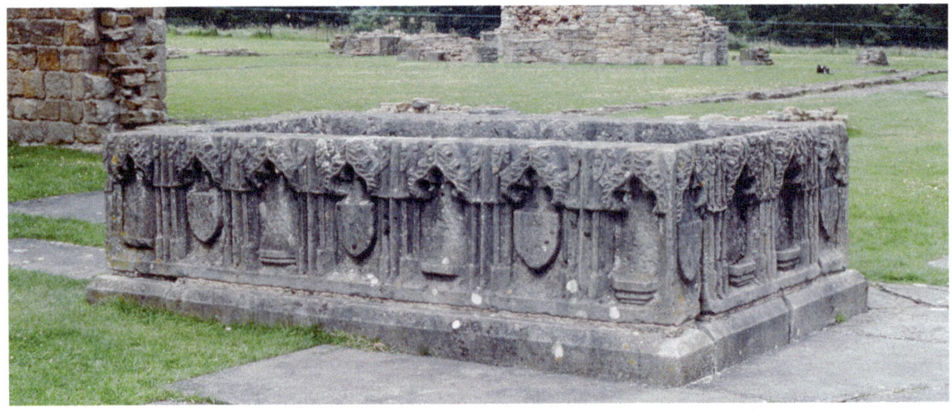

Egglestone Abbey (County Durham): tomb-chest commemorating Sir Ralph Bowes (died 1482) amid the ruins.

formed the core of a magnificent series of monuments to the Earls of Rutland. Some tombs were transferred to the nearby parish church, as with the alabaster effigies to Sir Thomas Fitzwillam (died 1478) and his first wife that were removed from the Austinfriars in Tickhill (South Yorkshire), or the brass of Geoffrey Barbur (died 1417), a merchant and benefactor of Abingdon (Oxfordshire), which was moved by the mayor and council from Abingdon Abbey to St Helen's church. Yet these were the exceptions. Monuments in parish churches did not escape the fury of the Reformation. The dissolution of the chantries and the iconoclasm that marked Edward VI's reign posed a great threat to them, particularly if inlaid with brass, which could be stripped out and sold for profit. Many monuments were mutilated; associated religious sculpture was the chief target but the faces and hands of effigies were also frequently damaged.

The Civil War also took its toll on monuments, both through deliberate iconoclasm and mindless vandalism, chiefly by Parliamentary

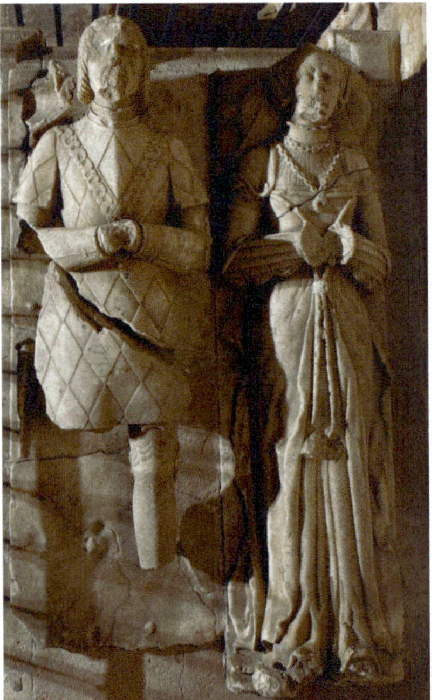

Tickhill (South Yorkshire). Sir Thomas Fitzwilliam (died 1478) and his first wife. This tomb was moved from Austinfriars to the parish church at the Reformation.

troops. Sir Humphrey Orme witnessed the smashing by soldiers of the wall monument that he had erected to his family in Peterborough Cathedral, as well as the destruction of other monuments, including to Queen Katherine of Aragon and Mary, Queen of Scots.

Although the Reformation and the Civil War resulted in the greatest destruction of tombs, they had always been under threat and were to remain so. Floor monuments were most at risk. New burials attracted fees for the church, and the presence of an existing monument in the chosen position was not necessarily a bar to reuse of the site. To quote again from *Piers the Plowman's Crede*, 'And in beldinge of tombes thei travaileth grete / To chargen her chirche-flore, and chaungen it ofte'. In the early fifteenth century a sacristan of Bury St Edmunds Abbey (Suffolk) was rebuked by the abbot for removing gravestones, 'thus setting a bad and pernicious example for all faithful Christians who wish, for the remedy of their souls, to place such stones over the tombs of predecessors, kinsmen and benefactors'. Yet documentary evidence shows that such reprimands had little lasting effect; avaricious church authorities remained eager for the income generated by the sale of old tombstones that had been cleared to make room for new burials.

In more recent centuries monuments have suffered as a result of church restorations, ignorance, accidents and theft. The eighteenth-century repaving of York Minster resulted in the destruction of over two hundred floor slabs, chiefly brasses and indents of lost brasses. In the early nineteenth century, a wooden effigy at Radcliffe-on-Trent (Nottinghamshire) was stolen by youths in 1809, then burnt on a bonfire to celebrate the death of Tom Paine, one of the American Founding Fathers. The attrition of Britain's monumental heritage continues to the present day. In 1977 a pair of wooden effigies was stolen from Hildersham (Cambridgeshire); they are now in a museum on the continent. The fine pair of wooden effigies commemorating Ralph Neville, second Earl of Westmorland (died 1484), and his wife, Margaret, at Brancepeth (County Durham) was consumed by fire in 1988. Most of an effigy of a lady of late-thirteenth- or early-fourteenth-century date from Etton (Yorkshire East Riding) was used as hardcore for a garage base in the 1980s. In the same decade cross-slabs from St Mary Redcliffe, Bristol, and incised slabs from St Botolph, Boston (Lincolnshire), were consigned to skips. Fortunately such instances are balanced by examples of local 'activists' who devote much time and effort in raising funds for the conservation of their monuments at risk. Long may they and their efforts prosper.

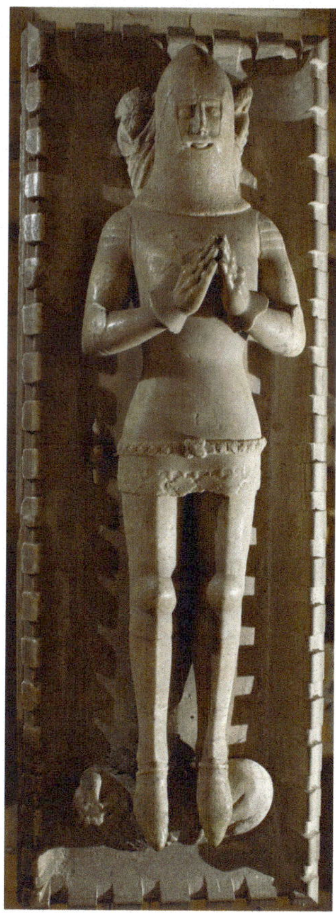

Bures, St Stephen's Chapel (Suffolk): Robert de Vere, fifth Earl of Oxford (died 1396). Originally in Colne Priory, this tomb was rescued, along with others to family members.

FURTHER READING

Badham, S. (with photography by M. Stuchfield). *Monumental Brasses*. Shire, 2009.

Badham, S., and Oosterwijk, S. (editors). *Monumental Industry: The Production of Tomb Monuments in England and Wales in the Long Fourteenth Century*. Shaun Tyas, 2010.

Crossley, F. H. *English Church Monuments AD 1150–1550*. Batsford, 1921.

Fryer, A. C. *Wooden Monumental Effigies in England and Wales*. Elliot Stock, 1924.

Gardner, A. *Alabaster Tombs of the Pre-Reformation Period in England*. CUP, 1940.

Greenhill, F. A. *Incised Effigial Slabs*. Faber & Faber, 1976.

Lindley, P. *Tomb Destruction and Scholarship. Medieval Monuments in Early Modern England*. Shaun Tyas, 2008.

Saul, N. *English Church Monuments in the Middle Ages. History and Representation*. OUP, 2009.

Tummers, H. *Early Secular Effigies in England: the Thirteenth Century*. Brill, 1980.

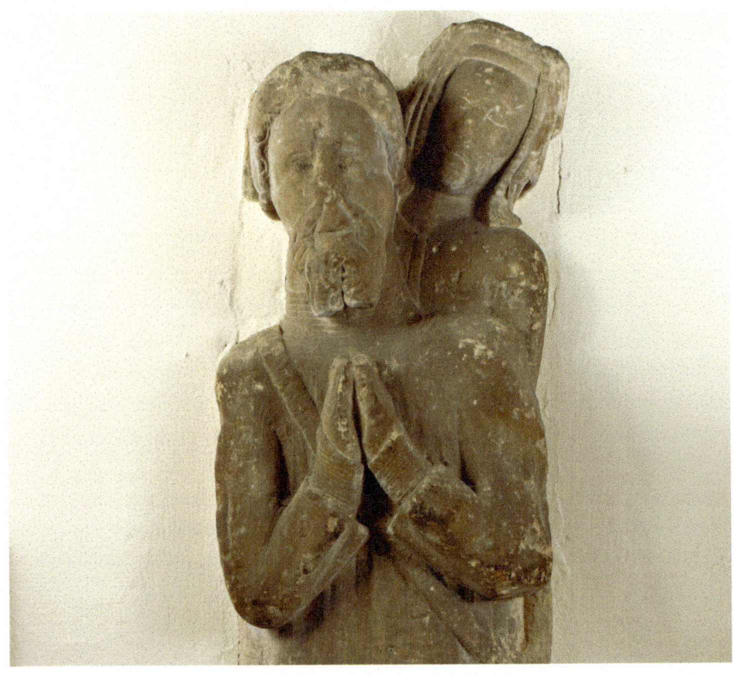

Ampleforth (North Yorkshire): a curious monument showing a bearded man of around 1330 with a lady peeping over his shoulder. The remains of an inscription have been plastered over.

PLACES TO VISIT

BEDFORDSHIRE
Cardington; Clifton; Goldingham; Luton; Salford; Turvey; Yeldon.
BERKSHIRE
Aldermaston; Aldworth; Barkham; Burghfield; Didcot; Englefield;
Sparsholt; Windsor, St George's Chapel.
BRISTOL (city and county)
Bristol, Cathedral, St Mark's Chapel, St Mary Redcliffe, St Stephen.
BUCKINGHAMSHIRE
Chilton; Clifton Reynes; Haversham; Hughenden; Leckhampstead;
Thornton.
CAMBRIDGESHIRE
(Italics: previously Huntingdonshire) Burrough Green; *Conington*;
Ely Cathedral; Fulbourn; *Great Staughton*; Little Shelford; *Orton
Longueville; Peterborough Cathedral; Ramsey Abbey*; Westley Waterless.
CHESHIRE
(Italics: previously Lancashire) Acton; Barthomley; Bunbury; Chester,
St John; Farndon; Macclesfield; Malpas; Over Peover; Rostherne;
Warrington.
CORNWALL
Bodmin; Callington; Cardinham; Duloe; Fowey; Lanivet; Phillack;
St Mawgan.
CUMBRIA
(Previously Cumberland, Lancashire and Westmorland) Appleby;
Calder Abbey; Carlisle Cathedral; Cartmel Priory; Furness Abbey;
Great Salkeld; Greystoke; Lanercost Priory; Lowther; Ousby.
DERBYSHIRE
Ashbourne; Bakewell; Chesterfield; Crich; Derby Cathedral;
Kedleston; Longford; Norbury; Radbourne; Scarcliffe; Swarkeston;
Tideswell; Wirksworth.
DEVON
Atherington; Axminster; Bere Ferrers; Colyton; Crediton; Exeter
Cathedral; Haccombe; Horwood; Landkey; Membury; Ottery St Mary;
Tawstock; West Down.
DORSET
Abbotsbury; Christchurch Priory; Dorchester; Glanvilles Wootton;
Horton; Puddletown; Sherborne Abbey; Tolpuddle; Trent; Wareham;
Wimborne Minster.
DURHAM
(Italics: previously in Yorkshire) Bishop Auckland, St Andrew;

Chester-le-Street; Durham Cathedral; Easington; Gainford; Hurworth;
Norton-on-Tees; Pittington; Redmarshall; Staindrop; Whitworth; *Wycliffe.*

ESSEX

Clavering; Danbury; Dunmow Priory; Faulkbourne; Halstead;
Layer Marney; Little Baddow; Little Horkesley; Little Leighs;
Stansted Montfitchet; Thorpe-le-Soken.

GLOUCESTERSHIRE

Berkeley; Coberley; English Bicknor; Frampton-on-Severn; Gloucester
Cathedral; Iron Acton; Leckhampton; Minchinhampton; Newland;
Old Sodbury; Pucklechurch; Shipton Moyne; Tetbury; Tewkesbury
Abbey; Winterbourne.

HAMPSHIRE

East Tisted; Monk Sherborne; Oakley; Romsey Abbey; Sopley;
Thruxton; Winchester Cathedral.

HEREFORDSHIRE

Abbey Dore; Allensmore; Clehonger; Croft; Edwyn Ralph; Hereford
Cathedral; Ledbury; Moccas; Much Marcle; Pembridge; Ross-on-Wye;
Welsh Bicknor; Weobley; Woolhope.

HERTFORDSHIRE

Aldenham; Brent Pelham; Eastwick; Flamstead; Little Munden;
St Albans Cathedral; Walkern.

ISLE OF WIGHT

Brading; Carisbrooke; Godshill.

KENT

Ash-near-Sandwich; Canterbury Cathedral; Faversham; Goudhurst;
Ickham; Ightham; Lydd; Minster-in-Sheppey; Penshurst; Rochester
Cathedral; Sandwich; Shorne.

LANCASHIRE

Caton; Heysham; Rufford.

LEICESTERSHIRE

Ashby-de-la-Zouch; Ashby Folville; Bottesford; Orton-on-the-Hill;
Prestwold; Rothley; Thurlaston; Tilton.

LINCOLNSHIRE

Burton Coggles; Buslingthorpe; Careby; Gosberton; Halton Holegate;
Heckington; Kingerby; Lincoln Cathedral; Little Steeping; Norton
Disney; Rand; Rippingale; Spilsby; Surfleet; Stoke Rochford; Sutterton.

LONDON, GREATER

(Italics: previously Surrey) *Beddington*; London, St Helen Bishopsgate;
Southwark Cathedral; Temple Church; Westminster Abbey.

MANCHESTER, GREATER

(Previously Lancashire or [italics] Cheshire) *Bowdon; Cheadle*; Rochdale,
St Chad; Standish; *Stockport, St Mary.*

MERSEYSIDE

(Previously Lancashire) Huyton; Sefton.

NORFOLK

Ashwellthorpe; Banham; Bircham Newton; East Harling;
East Tuddenham; Fersfield; Hingham; Ingham; Mautby; Reepham;
South Acre; Stratton Strawless; West Walton; Wickhampton.

NORTHAMPTONSHIRE

Alderton; Apethorpe; Ashton; Castle Ashby; Dodford; Gayton;
Hinton-in-the-Hedges; Lowick; Paulerspury; Rothwell; Spratton;
Stanford-on-Avon; Stowe-Nine-Churches; Sudborough; Towcester;
Warkworth.

NORTHUMBERLAND

Bothal; Cambo; Chillingham; Corsenside; Hexham Priory; Seaton
Delaval; Thockrington; Warkworth.

NOTTINGHAMSHIRE

Clifton; Fledborough; Gonalston; Holme-by-Newark; Holme
Pierrepont; Hoveringham; Laxton; Staunton-in-the-Vale; Strelley; West
Leake; Willoughby-on-the-Wolds; Wollaton.

OXFORDSHIRE

(Italics, previously Berkshire) Asthall; Broughton; Burford; Cogges;
Dorchester Abbey; Ewelme; Great Haseley; Little Wittenham; Minster
Lovell; North Leigh; Northmoor; Oxford Cathedral; Stanton Harcourt;
Wantage; Waterperry.

RUTLAND

Ashwell; Belton; Lyddington; Stoke Dry; Tickencote.

SHROPSHIRE

Albrighton; Berrington; Burford; Eaton-under-Haywood; Leighton;
Kinlet; Pitchford; Preston Gubbals; Shrewsbury, Abbey (Holy Cross),
St Mary; Tong; Whitchurch.

SOMERSET

Bathampton; Brympton d'Evercy; Chew Magna; Compton Martin;
Dunster; Farleigh Hungerford Castle chapel; Nettlecombe; Nunney;
Old Cleeve; Paulton; Porlock; South Petherton; Stogursey; Tickenham;
Wells Cathedral; Whatley.

STAFFORDSHIRE

Croxall; Draycott-in-the-Moors; Elford; Hanbury; Lichfield Cathedral;
Norbury; Tamworth; Trentham Park; Weston-under-Lizard.

SUFFOLK

Bures; Chilton; Dennington; Erwarton; Hawstead; Heveningham;
Kedington; Long Melford; Newton Green; Wingfield.

SURREY

Horley; Lingfield; Mickleham; West Horsley.

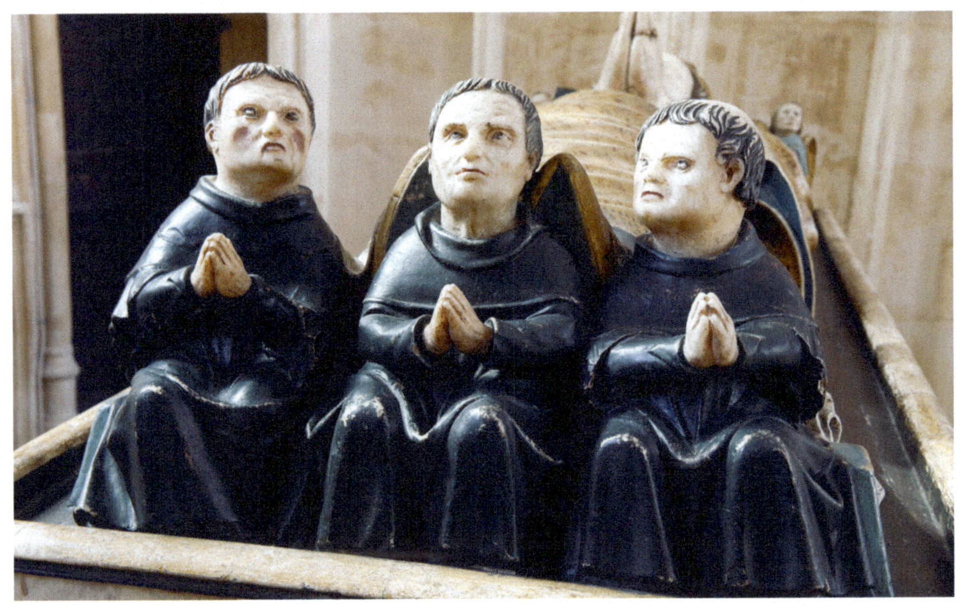

Winchester Cathedral (Hampshire): Bishop William of Wykeham (died 1404). Three monks, their heads being replacements, are shown at the foot of the effigy.

SUSSEX, EAST

Brede; Herstmonceux; Southover (Lewes); Winchelsea.

SUSSEX, WEST

Arundel; Boxgrove; Chichester Cathedral; Horsham; Ifield; West Wittering.

WARWICKSHIRE

Avon Dassett; Hillmorton; Merevale; Polesworth; Studley; Warwick, St Mary.

WEST MIDLANDS

(Previously Warwickshire) Aston; Hampton-in-Arden.

WILTSHIRE

Berwick St John; Boyton; Bradford-on-Avon; Britford; Broad Hinton; Bromham; Draycot Cerne; Edington; Great Bedwyn; Salisbury Cathedral; Sherston; Steeple Langford; Stockton; Tollard Royal; Winterbourne Bassett.

WORCESTERSHIRE

Bredon; Bromsgrove; Great Malvern; Kidderminster, St Mary; Pershore Abbey; Worcester Cathedral.

YORKSHIRE, EAST RIDING and CITY OF YORK

Bainton; Beverley Minster; Burton Agnes; Eastrington; Goxhill; Halsham; Harpham; Hornsea; Howden; Hull, Holy Trinity; Lowthorpe; Routh; Sutton-on-Hull; Swine; Welwick; York Minster.

YORKSHIRE, NORTH

Allerton Mauleverer; Bedale; Birkin; Brompton-in-Allertonshire;
Butterwick; Escrick; Felixkirk; Gilling East; Gilling West;
Goldsborough; Hazlewood Castle; Hornby; Kirkby Fleetham;
Nunnington; Pickering; Ripley; Ripon Cathedral; Ryther; West
Tanfield.

YORKSHIRE, SOUTH

Barnburgh; Fishlake; Loversall; Norton (Sheffield); South Anston;
Sprotbrough; Tickhill; Wadworth; Worsbrough.

YORKSHIRE, WEST

Batley; Dewsbury; Harewood; Kirkheaton; Methley; Thornhill.

WALES

Abergavenny; Bangor Cathedral; Brecon Cathedral; Coity; Coychurch;
Dolgellau; Ewenny; Flemingston; Gresford; Llanarmon-yn-Ial;
Llanbabo; Llanblethian; Llandaff Cathedral; Llandyfodwg; Llanfihangel
Abercywyn; Llaniestyn; Llantriddyd; Llantwit Major; Newborough;
Northop; Rhuddlan; Ruabon; Ruthin; St Asaph Cathedral; St Athan;
St Brides Major; St David's Cathedral; St Hilary; Tremeirchion; Valle
Crucis Abbey.

THE CHURCH MONUMENTS SOCIETY

The aims of the Church Monuments Society are to promote, for the
public benefit, the study, care and conservation of funerary monuments
of historical, artistic, architectural or educational importance, and
related art, of all periods and of all countries. Members receive the
annual journal *Church Monuments*, lavishly illustrated, including in
colour, and the *Newsletter*, published twice a year, with information
about current activities, work in progress and new literature. The lively
and varied meetings programme includes weekend symposia, study
days, coach excursions and other meetings, held in London and in the
regions.

Contacts: http://www.churchmonumentssociety.org or:
Church Monuments Society
c/o The Society of Antiquaries
Burlington House
Piccadilly
London
W1V 0HS.

Printed and bound by CPI Group (UK) Ltd, Croydon, CR0 4YY

14/05/2026

02110534-0002